Of Whom Do the Prophets Speak?

Messiah in the Prophecies

BY HOWARD MORGAN

Copyright © 2018 by Howard Morgan Ministries

All rights reserved. This book or any portion thereof may not be reproduced or used in any manner whatsoever without the express written permission of the publisher except for the use of brief quotations in a book review or scholarly journal.

First Printing: 2018

ISBN 978-1-329-19484-7

Edited by Deborah Boock, Michael Senger, Susan Gaines and Camille Montgomery.

Cover art created by Melanie Morgan and Michael Senger.

www.howardmorganministries.com

DEDICATION

This book is dedicated to all those whose lives have been changed by their encounter with the Jewish Messiah and who desire to share that experience and their understanding of how Jesus (Yeshua) is in fact the one "Of Whom the Prophets Speak."

ACKNOWLEDGEMENTS

Thanks to my beloved Jewish wife, Janet, whose life was changed by her encounter with the Jewish Messiah! To Camille Montgomery for her eye for details and perceptive questions. To Susan Gaines, my professional editor and good friend, who did what all good editors and friends do. Gentile women whose lives were also changed when they met the Jewish Messiah! May all your labors bear much fruit for the Kingdom of God!

TABLE OF CONTENTS

Dedication i
Acknowledgements ii
Introduction 1
   A Word To Our Jewish Friends: 1
   A Word To Our Christian Friends: 2
Chapter 1 – Atonement For Sin: The "Exchange Of Life" Principle 13
Chapter 2 – How To Identify The Messiah: A Study Of Messianic Prophecy 17
   The Hebrew Scriptures Give Us A Prophetic Picture Of The Messiah . 18
   The Place Of His Birth 18
   Messiah's Ancestry 22
Chapter 3 – Messiah's Ministry 29
Chapter 4 – Two Advents Of One Messiah Foretold By The Prophets 39
   The Purpose Of His First Coming 40
   The Second Coming Of The Messiah 42
   The Purpose Of His Second Coming Is To: 42
Chapter 5 – The Messiah: A Prophet, A Priest, And A King 47
   The Necessity Of A Prophet, Priest, And King 47
   The Prophet 47
   The Priest 48
   The King 51
Chapter 6 – Consider These Amazing Parallels Between The Life Of Moses And Jesus 55
Chapter 7 – Events Of Messiah's Betrayal, Death, Burial, Resurrection, And Ascension Foretold 63
Chapter 8 – Messiah Was To Be Rejected By The Jewish People 73
Chapter 9 – The Deity Of The Messiah 77
Chapter 10 – Evidence For The Resurrection Of Jesus From The Dead ... 89
Chapter 11 – Answering Some Common Jewish Objections To Jesus 93

Objection # 1: If You Believe In Jesus, You Stop Being Jewish!.........94

Objection # 2: Why Don't The Rabbis And The Jewish People Believe?...............98

Objection # 3: If Jesus Is The Messiah, Why Didn't He Bring Peace To The World?...............102

Objection # 4: I Am A Good Person, I Am Not A Sinner...................103

Objection # 5: I Don't Need A Mediator; I Can Approach God Directly...............104

Objection # 6: I Don't Need Your Messiah, I Already Pray And Admit My Sins To God. I Have My Own Religion. 106

Objection # 7: Why Have Christians Hated And Persecuted The Jews?...............106

Objection # 8: The New Testament Is An Anti-Semitic Book............107

Objection # 9: Why Are You Trying To Convert Us? We Have Our Own Religion! Preach To Your Own People! They Need It! 112

Objection # 10: How Can You Believe That The Bible Is The Word Of God? 113

Objection # 11: How Do You Know There Is Life After Death? 117

Objection # 12: What About Those Who Haven't Heard The Gospel? What About All The Virtuous Jewish People Who Don't Believe In Jesus?...............119

Objection # 13: If I Believe, Do I Have To Be Baptized?...................120

Chapter 12 – Some Guidelines For Sharing The Good News About Messiah Yeshua With The Jewish People 123

Chapter 13 – Explaining The Gospel To The Jewish People 133

Resources...............139

Contact Information...............140

Of Whom Do the Prophets Speak?

Messiah in the Prophecies

INTRODUCTION

A WORD TO OUR JEWISH FRIENDS:

This book is not about "converting Jews to Christianity." This book is not about changing your religion, rejecting beloved traditions or altering any part of your cultural identity as a Jew. It does not teach that Jews must leave their Synagogues, join a Church and become "Christians."

This book is built on the foundational understanding that revelatory encounters with God are at the heart of authentic Biblical "conversion." This supernatural experience with the Lord God of Israel is what the Patriarchs, true Prophets, Godly priests, Righteous Kings, and "ordinary" people, both Jews, and those from every nation throughout the ages, have also experienced.

This "conversion" is fundamentally not a change of "religion" but a change of one's relationship with God. It is a change of your spiritual reality. It is what the Hebrew word "Teshuva" – "Repentance" is all about. Teshuva means "turning" from and "turning" to. It is "turning" from spiritual darkness to light, from the guilt and negativity of sin to knowing the freedom of the forgiveness of those sins. It is "turning" from hopelessness to hope, from doubt to faith, from self-focused living to genuinely desiring to fulfill the will of God in all things. It is "turning" from life without God to life with God!

My motive for writing this book is twofold. First, it is to help people whose lives have been changed by their encounter with Jesus (Yeshua in Hebrew) to make a presentation to you about why they believe that Jesus is, in fact, the Jewish Messiah. This life-changing encounter creates a God given zeal to share with others the "Good News" of all that "Salvation in Jesus" means. They have discovered the "new life" that is promised in the Scriptures and made available by faith in the Messiah. My second motive is a desire to share with you those prophecies that I believe point to Yeshua in the Jewish Bible and ask you to consider "Of Whom Do the Prophets Speak?" Do they speak of Jesus, or someone else? If so, who might that be? Who else fulfills the prophecies?

The message of believers to you is essentially this: Your Messiah changed our lives. When we repented of our sins and received Yeshua as our Savior, Lord, and Messiah, your God, the God of Israel, the God of Abraham, Isaac, and Jacob assured us that our sins were forgiven. We have entered His "Spiritual Kingdom" and into a personal relationship with Him.

I have no desire to "convert" you to the Gentile religion of "Christianity." In fact, there are many Gentile believers in Jesus who understand the essential "Jewishness" of Jesus and the entire New Testament, or New Covenant Scriptures (terms I use interchangeably). They understand that it is they, as Gentiles, who have actually "converted" to a "Jewish religion." They have entered into a relationship with the God of Israel, study His Scriptures, and seek to live a life of faith and obedience to His commandments.

As Jews, my wife Janet and I were profoundly changed when we had supernatural encounters with the God of our Fathers, the God of Abraham, Isaac, and Jacob. He revealed to us that Yeshua/Jesus is, in fact, our Messiah.

Our hope and prayer is that you would prayerfully and seriously consider what you read here and not simply dismiss it. Ask the God of Israel if Jesus is really the Jewish Messiah. After all, it is only what He says that really matters, and His answer can change your life!

A WORD TO OUR CHRISTIAN FRIENDS:

To those who desire to share their faith in Jesus with the Jewish people an understanding of Jewish history is of utmost importance.

INTRODUCTION

Because the Jewish people suffered an almost 2,000-year history of "Christian" anti-Semitism and persecution, they developed a system of Scripture interpretation that eliminates Jesus from reasonable consideration as the Messiah. To see Jesus/Yeshua in the Hebrew Scriptures brings a Jewish person to a crisis of faith and religious/cultural identity. That revelation challenges the entire system of Jewish theology. It threatens the very identity and foundation of the "Jewishness" which has enabled the Jewish people to survive against the hate-filled onslaughts of those who claimed to represent "Christianity," as well as many other persecutors.

As you share the Gospel, you must understand that the Jewish people have their own way of interpreting the Scriptures in general, and Messianic Prophecy in particular. Some Jewish people and Rabbis will object to our understanding and interpretations of the Scriptures with accusations that we are "cherry-picking" verses that look like they apply to Jesus. Others will say that our Messianic interpretations are like "shooting an arrow and then drawing a bulls-eye around it."

Why, we must then ask, are there so many verses that can be "cherry-picked" or "encircled?" No other religious leaders or false messiahs can claim to have their life and ministry pre-written as prophecy in the Hebrew Scriptures. If they could, they would have certainly tried to use them as proof of the authenticity of their claims.

The reason there are so many verses that can be applied as evidence of Jesus' Messiahship is that they are fulfilled in Him. The truth is that all those verses, when connected, draw a very convincing picture that is seen clearly in the life and ministry of Yeshua. During His ministry, He often spoke of this, and after His resurrection, He "opened" the Scriptures to His disciples to explain how they spoke of Him.

Luke 24:25-27 *"O foolish men and slow of heart to believe in all that the prophets have spoken! Was it not necessary for the Messiah to suffer these things and to enter into His glory?" And beginning with Moses and with all the prophets, He explained to them the things concerning Himself in all the Scriptures."*

Luke 24:44-46 *"These are My words which I spoke to you while I was still with you, that all things which are written about me in the Law of Moses and the Prophets and the Psalms must be fulfilled." Then He opened their minds to understand the Scriptures, and He said to them, "Thus it is written, that the Messiah would suffer and rise again from the dead on the third day,"*

When sharing the Gospel with the Jewish people, you must be confident in the fact that the *"Gospel itself is the Power of God unto Salvation"* (Romans 1:16). The historical aberrant and counterfeit anti-Semitic "Church" never proclaimed the real life-giving Gospel of Salvation and Redemption to the Jewish people. The evil fruit of this Church is evidence that they never actually had it themselves.

What they did have, and what they did seek to violently force upon the Jewish people, was an aberrant "Christianized" religion that was a mixture of Greek Humanistic Philosophy, Roman "Emperor" style oppressive leadership, and Pagan beliefs. This "Church" was demonically inspired to violently demand that the Jews "convert" to their "religion" and renounce and reject anything and everything that made them "Jewish."

But the Jewish people knew (and still know - even if they don't believe it) that their God revealed Himself at Mt. Sinai when He made His Covenant with them and gave them His Torah (the first five books of the Hebrew Bible). I believe that at that moment God put an eternal identity as "Jews" deep within their DNA. Even if individuals don't believe in God, or are not at all religious, because of the supernatural nature of that Covenant they have a deep inner identity that they are "Jews." God has determined that the Jewish people are *"chosen to be a people for His own possession"* and that they are to be *"a distinct people, not reckoned among the nations"* (Deuteronomy 14:2; Numbers 23:9).

What would you have done (or would do today) in the face of persecution and death? Would you affirm your commitment to the covenantal promises of God in your own Holy Scriptures or would you "convert" to a foreign religion? Would you obey the "Sword of the Spirit" (the *Word of God*) or the Sword of Steel? Facing these tremendous pressures there were Jewish people who would not "convert," even as others accepted that fate. The Rabbis built a theology to prove the erroneousness of the "Christianity" forced upon them and established as a fundamental principle of Judaism a continual rejection of "Jesus" as a false Messiah.

However, the Scriptures remain true no matter how badly the Church has acted. The Hebrew Scriptures do proclaim the coming of the Messiah and how we can identify Him.

Understanding the Words "Missionaries" and "Conversion"

"Missionaries" and "Conversion" are two of the most powerfully negative words to the Jewish people. To them, a missionary is "someone who wants to convert us to Christianity and make us into Gentiles." Some even refer to missionaries as "soul-stealers." Conversion, or even considering Jesus as the Messiah, is believed to be an act of religious and spiritual "high treason." A Jew who believes in Jesus is considered an apostate, a heretic, an idolater, and a "Meshumad" – a term that means a betrayer of his people. To "convert" is to reject your own "Jewishness," i.e., your religion, history, traditions, and culture, as well as your family, friends and the entire Jewish nation. In short, you become a goy (a Gentile).

The Jewish people also see "conversion" as a betrayal of their ancestors because you are joining the religion that was not only their historical persecutors' and murderers', but the religion that was also responsible for the Holocaust, either directly by perpetrators who claimed to be "Christians" or indirectly by the Church's acquiescence and silence.

To most Jews "conversion" is not an option. There is nothing about "Christianity" that is attractive, and its history toward the Jewish people is detestable. To the Christian, the Jewish person would say, "You have your religion; we have ours. You have your Bible; we have ours. You have your Pastors or Priests; we have our Rabbis. You have your Churches; we have our Synagogues. You have your holidays; we have ours. You have your beliefs; we have ours. Your religion is for the Gentiles; our religion is for the Jews. You have nothing we need or want, so please enjoy your religion and leave us alone."

This kind of thinking reflects their understanding of "conversion" as changing religion, not one's relationship with God Himself. It also reflects the deeply rooted sense of Jewish identity that is found even among the most secular, agnostic or even atheistic Jewish person who will say: "I was born a Jew, and I will die a Jew!" Whatever being a "Jew" means to them.

While there are many ways that Jews maintain their sense of identity and have varieties of opinions on just about every issue, Jewish people have universal agreement on these major issues:

- ✡ The survival of the Jewish people and the nation of Israel is paramount.
- ✡ There must never again be a Holocaust.
- ✡ "Christianity" is for the Gentiles.
- ✡ Jesus is not our Messiah, and He is not divine.

If the Jewish people accuse you of wanting to "convert" them, you must be very clear in explaining your motives. Tell them that you are motivated by the redemptive Love of God that has changed your life. Explain that it is the Jewish Scriptures that teach that the Jewish Messiah is the sin-bearer for Jew and Gentile alike and that faith in the Jewish Messiah doesn't *diminish* one's Jewishness but enhances it because it opens the door to a personal relationship with the God of Israel. Share how the Lord has inspired you to share the life-changing message of God's offer of Salvation and Redemption in the Jewish Messiah. If they say that Jesus is not the Jewish Messiah, you can tell him that God promised the Messiah to only one people, the Jews, and there is no such thing as a "Gentile Messiah." Then you might ask if they know what the Hebrew Prophets said about the Messiah. This might open a door for you to share some Messianic prophecies with them. You might also mention that we can consider Abraham the first "missionary" because he was called to bring the message of the "One True God" to the world.

INTRODUCTION

Explain that you understand all the negative things attached to the word "conversion" and that you are not talking about any of them. In fact, we are not talking about religion at all. All religions are human attempts to reach God through various kinds of self-effort. Rabbis often talk about prayer, studying the Torah and Talmud (Rabbinic commentaries), doing good works, keeping the Sabbath and eating only kosher food, as ways to "merit" God's favor and blessings. You can share the New Covenant teaching that no one can ever be "good enough" or "do enough good works" to "merit" or "earn" salvation. Explain that salvation and eternal life is the "free gift of God's grace" to all who turn from their sins and receive Yeshua as Lord and Savior (Romans 6:23; Ephesians 2:8).

Explain that "conversion" refers to the Hebrew word "Teshuva," which can also be translated, "Repentance" or "Turning." Make clear that real Biblical conversion is a supernaturally inspired transformation of heart that changes someone's personal relationship with God and has nothing to do with changing religions or rejecting one's heritage, culture or people. This supernatural work of God imparts a desire to repent of their sins, turn away from a self-focused lifestyle and creates an aspiration to live a life of faithful obedience to God's will.

Becoming a Jewish believer in Jesus does not mean giving up anything about one's "Jewishness." Rather, the believer enters a personal relationship with God, gains the sure knowledge of the forgiveness of their sins, and has the opportunity to receive the gift of the Holy Spirit. This is the very first message the Jewish Apostle Peter preached to the Jewish people gathered at the Temple in Jerusalem to celebrate the festival of Shavuot (Pentecost). Under the anointing of the Holy Spirit, he told the crowd to *"Turn from sin (repent), return to God, and each of you be immersed (baptized) on the authority of Yeshua the Messiah (in the name of Jesus Christ) for the forgiveness of your sins, and you will receive the gift of the Ruach HaKodesh (the Holy Spirit)!"* (Acts 2:38).

Real Biblical conversion brings us into a wonderful life-changing personal relationship with the God of Abraham, Isaac, and Jacob that produces an abundant life of peace, purpose, meaning, and joy.

Explain that it's not what they give up; it's what they gain! This might be a great place to share what God has done in your own life.

Psalm 51:10-13 and Ezekiel 36:24-28 express what Biblical conversion is most poignantly:

"Create in me a clean heart, O God, and renew a steadfast spirit within me.
Do not cast me away from your presence and do not take your Holy Spirit from me.
Restore to me the joy of your salvation and sustain me with a willing spirit.
Then I will teach transgressors your ways, and sinners will be turned (converted) to you."

"For I will take you from among the nations, gather you from all the countries, and return you to your own soil. Then I will sprinkle clean water on you, and you will be clean; I will cleanse you from all your uncleanness and from all your idols. I will give you a new heart and put a new spirit inside you;
I will take the stony heart out of your flesh and give you a heart of flesh. I will put My Spirit inside you and cause you to live by My laws, respect My rulings and obey them.
You will live in the land I gave to your ancestors. You will be My people, and I will be your God."

Just Be a Witness

The Bible says that we ought to be able to make a *"defense of the hope that is within us"* (1 Peter 3:15). As *"able ministers of the Spirit"* (2 Corinthians 3:6) we should be able to explain why we believe that the Messianic prophecies of the Hebrew Scriptures identify Yeshua as the Messiah. Even as we share the Scriptures, we must always be sensitive to the leading of the Holy Spirit.

Remember that Yeshua said that no one would be able to believe in Him unless God revealed to them that He was the Messiah.

INTRODUCTION

"Jesus answered and said to him, "Blessed are you, Simon Bar Jonah, because flesh and blood did not reveal this to you, but My Father who is in heaven." (Matthew 16:17).

"No one can come to Me, unless the Father who sent Me draws him; and I will raise him up on the last day." (John 6:44)

"He was saying, "For this reason I have said to you, that no one can come to Me, unless it has been granted him from the Father." (John 6:65)

May the Lord make us all people of wisdom and power as we share the Messiah with God's "Chosen People" (Deuteronomy 7:6-8).

If your witness about Jesus encounters resistance or rejection, don't be troubled by it. Your job is not to convince anyone of the truth of the Gospel. Only the Holy Spirit can bring revelation about who Jesus really is. You have not been called to be a "soul-winner," because only God can "win souls"!

When Proverbs 11:30 speaks of the "wise winning (or literally "taking") souls," it means a wise life is lived to help others in their spiritual journey. The picture I see is taking someone by the hand and escorting them toward God.

People who misunderstand this and think of themselves as a "soul-winner," make the mistake of believing it is their responsibility to "convince" someone to believe. They set themselves up for unnecessary disappointment and frustration. We are not the "soul-winner." God has not called you, anointed you, or made you to be a "soul winner." That is His job. Your job is simply to be a witness of your faith in Jesus, to testify of what He has done in your life and share what the Scriptures proclaim. This is what the Lord has called and anointed you to do.

If people reject your testimony, that is simply none of your business. In a court of law, the witness is not upset if the jury doesn't believe him. He is not upset if the attorneys, the judge, or the spectators don't believe him. He simply says, "Believe it or not, that's what happened, that's what I witnessed. If you don't want to believe me, that's your choice, but I know what I know." This should be your attitude as you share your faith with Jewish people. Show them the Love of God and move on to the next person who may be open to your testimony.

The blind man who was healed by the Lord Jesus in John chapter 9 was not troubled by the furor that his healing caused. He was healed! He could see! That was the only thing that mattered. He said in effect to his interrogators, "You've got problems with Jesus? Go to Him; I was blind, now I can see! Have you theological problems with Jesus being the Messiah? Go straighten them out with Him. All I can tell you is that He healed me! This may be a problem for you, but it is not a problem for me! Hallelujah, I can SEE!"

This story is a powerful lesson for us. What this man exemplified should be our attitude toward everyone we witness to. If someone has a problem with your faith in the Lord Jesus, and your testimony of what He has done in your life, that is their problem, not yours. You go on your way rejoicing! Don't lose any sleep because someone is upset with you. Don't be bothered because of other people's responses to your witness. Just smile, love them and pray for them! Who knows how the Lord can use your witness sometime in the future? Perhaps He will use it to convict them of their sins and bring them to faith.

It is very important that you properly respond to their resistance and rejection. Do not let any negative thoughts and feelings fill your soul. Those negative thoughts and the negative feelings they create (like bitterness, resentment, and unforgiveness), are open doors for demonic lies that will only exacerbate those thoughts and feelings (2 Corinthians 2:11). *"Guard your heart,"* says Proverbs 4:23, because *"out of it springs forth the issues of life."* You only want love, and all the wonderfully positive things love produces, like peace and joy, to spring forth both into and out of your life! Amen!

Allow me to share a personal story. When I first became a believer, I shared the story of my encounter with the Lord with my friends. One of the gals was particularly hostile in her response to me. A few years later I got a phone call from her. She was inquiring about my faith. At first, I thought it was a prank. Then she said to me, "You're the only true believer I have ever met," and started asking me sincere questions. I had the privilege of "leading" her to the Lord, and she was baptized soon after that.

Why Do You Want to Go to Heaven?

When we pastored a congregation in Brooklyn, New York, we had weekly summer street evangelistic outreaches. Occasionally a Jewish person would engage us in conversation, and some were very adamant that they were going to Heaven. As I heard them say this, something was stirred in my spirit, so I started seeking the Lord about it. He said to me, "Why don't you ask them why they want to go to Heaven? What do they expect to find there? Ask them if they love to worship God now? Do they love to pray? Do they love to study God's Word? Do they love to talk about God and learn about God now? If they don't love those things now, why do they want to go to Heaven?" I remember thinking, wow what a good answer! I knew it had not come from me!

I prayed that during our next outreach another Jewish person would tell me that they were going to Heaven. God answered My prayer when a group of Jewish people stopped to talk to us at our literature table. One of the women, again, very adamantly and confidently said that she was going to Heaven. I said, "Oh, that's great," but why do you want to go there?" They all looked at me very quizzically because no one had ever asked them that. I said, "What do you think you will find in Heaven?" Do you love to worship God now? Do you love to talk to God now? Do you love to talk about God? That's what is going on in Heaven right now. Heaven is filled with people who love to express their love for God by singing to Him, listening to Him, and talking with each other about Him." Are you sure you want to go to Heaven? Are you sure you're going to like it? If you don't like doing those things now, what makes you think you're going to like it then?" They all looked at me stone-faced and slowly walked away. I knew I had given them something to think about.

People like to think they are going to Heaven. That's fine; they can think whatever they like. But asking them these kinds of questions will prove to be very enlightening. I have heard Jewish people tell me after I asked these questions, "Well I guess I will go to hell where all My friends are." These questions cause people to realize that they do not like doing the kinds of things they will be "forced" to do in Heaven. Heaven certainly would not be Heaven for them.

CHAPTER 1 – ATONEMENT FOR SIN: THE "EXCHANGE OF LIFE" PRINCIPLE

Leviticus 17:11 *"...the life of the flesh is in the blood: and I have given it to you upon the altar to make an atonement for your souls; for it is the blood that makes an atonement for the soul."*

Hebrews 9:22 *"...without shedding of blood there is no forgiveness."*

Matthew 26:28 *"Jesus said, "This is My blood of the New Covenant, which is shed for many for the remission of sins."*

2 Corinthians 5:21 *"He made Him who knew no sin to be sin on our behalf, that we might become the righteousness of God in Him."*

The Rabbis teach that since the Temple was destroyed and sacrifices ceased to be offered, now these are sufficient substitutes for the blood of the sacrifices:

- ✡ Study of the Torah and the Talmud (Rabbinic Commentaries).
- ✡ Prayer.
- ✡ Repentance.
- ✡ Good Deeds.
- ✡ Fasting on Yom Kippur.

But are they adequate to deal with sin? Do they really make atonement? In Isaiah 64:6, God says that all our "good works" are as "filthy rags." When we trust that our "good works" make us righteous before the Lord, we make an error that can have eternal consequences!

If prayer, repentance and good deeds were sufficient to atone for sins, why would God have required blood sacrifices in the first place? He wouldn't have. Because our "good works" cannot make atonement for our sins, God created a way for us to receive atonement. The entire sacrificial system of the Torah, the Levitical priesthood, the Temple and the detailed instructions for sacrifices, all show the way that Israel's sins were to be forgiven. This system of sacrifice is built upon the "Exchange of Life" principle.

The "Exchange of Life" principle reflects the fundamental understanding that each person recognizes that their-sins need an atoning sacrifice. They believed that the sacrificial animal was their personal substitute. When they presented their offering, they laid their hands upon the head of the animal and confessed their sins, which were then, by faith, imputed or transferred to the sacrifice. The animal then took on the sins of the individual. Slaying the animal and seeing its shed blood was a very graphic lesson about the penalty for sin being death (Leviticus 1:3-5; 4:5). It also clearly shows us the mercy of God who provides a substitute to die in place of the repentant sinner. Here is the "Exchange of Life." The innocent sacrifice takes on the sin and dies, and the repentant sinner receives forgiveness and life.

God did not leave the Jewish people without an atoning sacrifice after the destruction of the Temple and Priesthood in 70 A.D. Daniel and Isaiah prophesied that the Messiah would fulfill the "Exchange of Life" principle. He would be *"cut off,"* and *"make atonement."* He would be *"pierced for our transgressions,"* *"crushed for our iniquities,"* *"bring healing by His wounds,"* and *"bear the sin of many"* (Daniel 9:24-26; Isaiah 53:5, 12).

The revelation of the New Covenant is that a new Priesthood was established, and an eternal Atoning Sacrifice was made. Messiah Yeshua/Jesus, *"a priest after the order of Melchizedek"* (Psalm 110:4; Hebrews 5:6-10; 6:20; 7:1-17) became "sin for us" (2 Corinthians 5:21). By faith in His atoning blood (Romans 3:25) our sins are forgiven (Colossians 1:14). By faith, His righteousness is imparted to us and becomes our own (Romans 3:22; 4:5; 5:9; Philippians 3:9).

Beloved reader, take some time to meditate on these verses. If they are not already spiritually alive in your life, please seek the Lord for a revelation of their reality. Once they become real for you, you will never be the same!

CHAPTER 1 – ATONEMENT FOR SIN: THE "EXCHANGE OF LIFE" PRINCIPLE

We see the power of "Sacrificial blood" in the Passover story. A lamb was slain, and its blood applied to the entrance of each home. When the Lord saw the blood He *"passed over"* the house. It was not enough that it was a Jewish home. That home had to have blood on the top of the door frame and each door post (Exodus 12:21-24). Similarly, on Yom Kippur - The Day of Atonement, the High Priest entered the Holy of Holies and placed atoning blood on the Mercy Seat assuring forgiveness for the nation (Leviticus 16).

- In Leviticus 1 - The blood of the sin offerings provided atonement for individuals.

- In Exodus 12 - The blood of the Passover Lamb provided protection for families.

- In Leviticus 16 - The blood of the Yom Kippur sacrifice provided atonement for the nation.

- In Isaiah 53 - The blood of Messiah's sacrifice provided atonement for the world.

The Hebrew word for "atonement" (Kippur) carries the meaning of "ransom by providing a substitute." The entire sacrificial system was created to remove sin by the sacrifice of an innocent life. Why did God create this system of sacrifice? He wants us to see the absolute awfulness of sin and its consequences. Sin always brings death (Ezekiel 18:4, 20; Romans 5:12; 6:16, 23).

The sacrifice also clearly showed:

1) God's Holiness - His absolute hatred of evil.

2) God's Justice - He doesn't leave sin unpunished.

3) God's Mercy - His readiness to pardon the truly repentant person by providing a substitute.

Repentance (confessing and turning away from sin) and faith (trusting God to forgive) must be present for this "Exchange of Life" principle to work (Psalm 51:17, 19). <u>Remember, repentance and faith alone are not enough, the shedding of sacrificial blood is required.</u> We cannot offer to God those things we conceive ourselves and believe, even if this is what our religious leaders teach and to which everyone agrees. They are counterfeit substitutes for what He has commanded in the Scriptures and are unacceptable to Him.

CHAPTER 2 – HOW TO IDENTIFY THE MESSIAH: A STUDY OF MESSIANIC PROPHECY

This section contains a compilation of material that will be a very good beginning in your study of Messianic prophecy. I also have included some of the controversies and objections that are commonly found when witnessing to the Jewish people. I have given you some answers to use so that you will be able to *"give a reasoned answer to anyone who asks you to explain the hope you have in you"* (1 Peter 3:15).

As you become familiar with this material, you will be well on your way to become an effective witness for Jesus to the Jewish people. For further study refer to the resources listed at the end of this book.

Remember that the Gospel is a supernatural story and must be presented like that. As you study these prophecies, pray that God will give you His understanding and put His love and passion in your heart. The last thing the Jewish people need is loveless Christians trying to coerce them with Biblical "proof texts." 1 Corinthians 13:1 teaches us that knowledge without love is like a *"clanging cymbal."* Imagine yourself standing next to someone as they clang symbols together right next to your head. Not a very pleasant thought and certainly something you would stop. Witnessing to the Jewish people without love is just like that. They don't hear the Lord; they hear *"clanging symbols."*

Ask the Lord to fill you with His Love for His Ancient Covenant people. When the Holy Spirit empowers you with His Love, your whole life will change. Not only will you love the Jewish people, but you will also love all people!

May God grant you love and wisdom as you study and share the One who has changed your life!

In each of the following sections, you will see the Messianic Prophecies and the New Covenant fulfillment.

THE HEBREW SCRIPTURES GIVE US A PROPHETIC PICTURE OF THE MESSIAH

Psalm 40:7 *"Then I said, "Behold, I come; In the Scroll of the Book it is written of Me"*

Luke 24:44 *"These are My words which I spoke to you while I was still with you, that all things which are written about me in the Law of Moses and the Prophets and the Psalms must be fulfilled."*

THE PLACE OF HIS BIRTH

The Ruler of Israel Was to Be Born in Bethlehem

Micah 5:2 *"But as for you, Bethlehem Ephratah, too little to be among the clans of Judah, from you One will go forth for me to be the ruler of Israel. His goings forth are from long ago, from the days of eternity."*

Matthew 2:1 *"Now after Jesus was born in Bethlehem of Judea in the days of Herod the King, behold, Magi from the east arrived in Jerusalem."*

The Miraculous Circumstances of His Birth

Isaiah 7:14 *"Therefore the Lord Himself shall give you a sign; Behold, a virgin shall conceive, and bear a son, and shall call His name Immanuel."*

Matthew 1:22-23 *"Now all this took place that what was spoken by the Lord through the prophet might be fulfilled, saying," "Behold, the virgin shall be with child, and shall bear a Son, and they shall call His name Immanuel," which translated means, "God with us."*

CHAPTER 2 – HOW TO IDENTIFY THE MESSIAH: A STUDY OF MESSIANIC PROPHECY

Matthew's insightful interpretation of Isaiah's prophecy reflects his tenure as one of Jesus' disciples. Not only did Jesus open this verse to them and explain its Messianic meaning, but they all knew Miriam (Mary), Jesus' mother, and learned from her the story of His conception and birth. This is why Matthew can apply this verse to Jesus' birth as a miraculous sign and its fulfillment as a Messianic prophecy. Furthermore, the child born of the virgin was to have a divine nature. He is called *"Immanuel,"* which means *"God with us."*

There is some controversy over the Hebrew word "Almah" translated "virgin" in Isaiah 7:14. The Rabbis say that Almah does not mean "virgin," but that the Hebrew word Betulah means "virgin." However, Almah can mean "a young woman who is a virgin." In Genesis 24:43, Rebekah is described as a virgin (Almah). In Song of Solomon 1:3 and 6:8, we find Almot, the plural of Almah, translated as "virgins." The other word for virgin is Betulah, but in Joel 1:8 it refers to a widow who was of course at one time a married woman and would no longer be a virgin. The word Almah appears seven times in the Old Testament[1] and is translated "virgin," "damsel," and "maid."

The Jewish scholars who translated the Hebrew Bible into Greek about 250 years before the birth of Jesus, (this translation is known as the Septuagint for the seventy scholars who did the work) translated the Hebrew word Almah into the Greek word Parthenos, which means "virgin." They obviously did not have a "Christian" bias. They translated what the text simply said. The verse predicted a miraculous act of God which would be the sign. Isaiah 7:14 speaks of "a sign" to give special attention to this birth. The Hebrew word for sign used here is the same word used in Isaiah 38:7-8 to describe the miraculous turning back of the shadow on the sundial for King Hezekiah and is the same word used in Exodus 4:8-9 to describe the many miraculous signs given to Pharaoh through Moses. It is obviously no "sign" for a woman to give birth, but for a virgin to conceive and give birth would indeed be a miraculous "sign."

---

[1] Genesis 24:43, Exodus 2:8, Psalms 68:25, Proverbs 30:19, Song of Solomon 1:3 and 6:8, and Isaiah 7:14.

The child born of this miracle is to be called *Immanuel*, which means "God with us." Certainly, someone who is described as God could have such a miraculous birth.

The Time of Messiah's Appearing

Daniel 9:24-27
"Seventy weeks have been decreed for your people and your holy city, to finish the transgression, to make an end of sin, to make atonement for iniquity, to bring in everlasting righteousness, to seal up vision and prophecy, and to anoint the most Holy Place." "So, you are to know and discern that from the issuing of a decree to restore and rebuild Jerusalem until Messiah the Prince there will be seven weeks and sixty-two weeks; it will be built again, with plaza and moat, even in times of distress. Then after the sixty-two weeks the Messiah will be cut off and have nothing, and the people of the prince who is to come will destroy the city and the sanctuary. Its end will come with a flood; even to the end there will be war; desolations are determined. He will make a firm covenant with the many for one week, but in the middle of the week he will put a stop to sacrifice and grain offering; and on the wing of abominations will come one who makes desolate, even until a complete destruction, one that is decreed, is poured out on the one who makes desolate."

The seven "weeks" in Hebrew says seven "Shavuim." The word "Shavuim" here refers to a "week" of seven years, as Daniel is writing about the 70 years of Babylonian captivity. From the time of the decree to rebuild Jerusalem to the time of Messiah is 7 weeks of years + 62 weeks of years = 69 weeks of years, or 69 x 7 = 483 years. (We still have one more prophetic "week of years" (seven years) yet to be fulfilled before Messiah's return).

Nehemiah 2:1-8 gives the account of Artaxerxes' granting permission to rebuild the Temple and Jerusalem. This happened "in the 20th year of King Artaxerxes' reign," which was 455 BC. If we count off 483 years from our starting point of 455 BC, we arrive at the year 29. This is the year Jesus of Nazareth began his ministry.

CHAPTER 2 – HOW TO IDENTIFY THE MESSIAH: A STUDY OF MESSIANIC PROPHECY

Daniel's prophecy also states that Messiah had to come and *"make atonement for iniquity"* by being *"cut off and have nothing."* To be *"cut off"* means He would be killed. This was all to happen before the *"people of the prince who is to come will destroy the city and the sanctuary."* This refers to the Roman general Titus who destroyed Jerusalem and the Temple in 70 AD. So, we see that the Messiah had to come before the Second Temple was destroyed.

The facts revealed in this extraordinary prophecy show that:

1) The time of the Messiah's appearance was clearly predetermined.

2) That time was before the Second Temple was destroyed.

3) The Messiah had to be killed.

These facts present some of the strongest evidence that the Messiah had to appear before 70 AD. Only Jesus did that, and it is too late for anyone else to do it.

There are Jewish traditions that discourage the study of the Book of Daniel because the Rabbis fear that people can be misled as they try to understand when the Messiah would come.

Genesis 49:10
"The scepter shall not depart from Judah, nor the ruler's staff from between His feet, until Shiloh comes, and to Him shall be the obedience of the peoples."

The scepter is the symbol of tribal rulership. This prophecy declares that the scepter shall not depart, or Judah's ruling authority shall not end, until "Shiloh" comes. The word "Shiloh" means "whose right it is" or "to whom it belongs," with "it" meaning authority. There is general agreement among Christian scholars and Rabbis that the term "Shiloh" denotes the Messiah. The Targums (Jewish Amplified Bibles) agree with this, as does the Peshitta (The Syriac Version of the Bible) which translates it as "to whom the Kingdom belongs."

Rashi, the foremost medieval Rabbinic interpreter of Scripture, says that Shiloh is "King Messiah."

The tribal authority of Judah came to an end when the Temple was destroyed. According to this prophecy, Shiloh (Messiah) had to come before that event. He did!

The Jewish apostle Paul writes in Galatians 4:4-5 about the time of the Messiah's appearing: *"But when the fullness of the time came, God sent forth His Son, made of a woman, made under the law, to redeem them that were under the law, that we might receive the adoption of sons."*

John 4:25-26 *"The woman said to Him, "I know that Messiah is coming... when that One comes, He will declare all things to us. Jesus said to her, "I who speak to you am He."*

Romans 1:1-4 *"Paul, a bond-servant of Messiah Yeshua, called as an Apostle, set apart for the Gospel of God, which He promised beforehand through His prophets in the Holy Scriptures, concerning His Son, who was born of a descendant of David according to the flesh, who was declared the Son of God with power by the resurrection from the dead, according to the Spirit of Holiness, Messiah Yeshua, our Lord,"*

Messiah's Ancestry

Messiah to Be the Descendant of Eve Who Will Destroy Satan

Genesis 3:15 *"And I will put enmity between you and the woman, and between your seed and her seed; He shall bruise you on the head, and you shall bruise him on the heel."*

When Rabbi Saul, (who would become the Apostle Paul) had his divine revelatory encounter that brought him to faith that Jesus was the Messiah, Jesus said these words to him:

CHAPTER 2 – HOW TO IDENTIFY THE MESSIAH: A STUDY OF MESSIANIC PROPHECY

"Arise, and stand on your feet; for this purpose I have appeared to you, to appoint you a minister and a witness not only to the things which you have seen but also to the things in which I will appear to you; delivering you from the Jewish people and from the Gentiles, to whom I am sending you, to open their eyes so that they may turn from darkness to light and from the dominion of Satan to God, in order that they may receive forgiveness of sins and an inheritance among those who have been sanctified by faith in Me" (Acts 26:16-18).

Here we gain the understanding that when our spiritual eyes are opened, and we have faith in Jesus, Satan's "head is bruised." That is, we are freed from his controlling influence and can *"turn from darkness to light and from the dominion of Satan to God."* When we do this, we receive the *"forgiveness of sins"* and a new spiritual *"inheritance"* with all those who also believe.

If you want to learn more about this "spiritual inheritance," you can begin with studying these verses:

>   Galatians 3:18; Ephesians 1:11, 14, 18; 5:5; Colossians 1:12; 3:24; Hebrews 9:15; 11:8; 1 Peter 1:4.

When this great Jewish Apostle wrote his letter to the believers in the city of Colossae, (in modern day Turkey), he explained further how Jesus "bruised Satan's head." He taught us that: "*He (God) made you alive together with Him (Jesus), having forgiven us all our transgressions, having canceled out the certificate of debt consisting of decrees against us and which was hostile to us; and He (God) has taken it out of the way, having nailed it to the cross. When He had disarmed the (demonic) rulers and authorities, He made a public display of them, having triumphed over them through it*" (Colossians 2:13-15).

Through Jesus' atoning death our sins are forgiven, and satanic *"rulers and authorities"* are now *"disarmed."* Jesus' scourging at the hands of the Roman soldiers and the suffering He endured in His crucifixion was His *"heel"* being bruised. That same suffering, by providing atonement for sin, *"bruised"* Satan's head. It broke his spiritual authority over the life of anyone who believes in Jesus.

Having been *"disarmed"* in this way, believers can now exercise spiritual authority over him in their spiritual battles (see also these New Testament verses: Ephesians 6:10-18; 2 Corinthians 2:11; 6:7; 10:4; 1 Peter 5:8-9; James 4:7).

Because we still must carry out the victory Jesus has won, we are in daily spiritual battles. To achieve personal spiritual victory, we must follow the instructions the Apostle Paul gave us in Ephesians 6:10-17, *"Finally, be strong in the Lord, and in the strength of His might. Put on the full armor of God, that you may be able to stand firm against the schemes of the devil. For our struggle is not against flesh and blood, but against the rulers, against the powers, against the world forces of this darkness, against the spiritual forces of wickedness in the heavenly places. Therefore, take up the full armor of God, that you may be able to resist in the evil day, and having done everything, to stand firm. Stand firm therefore, having girded your loins with truth, and having put on the breastplate of righteousness, and having shod your feet with the preparation of the gospel of peace; in addition to all, taking up the shield of faith with which you will be able to extinguish all the flaming missiles of the evil one. And take the helmet of salvation, and the sword of the Spirit, which is the word of God."*

Our spiritual battles will continue until the day Satan, and all his demonic underlings, are finally destroyed in the Lake of Fire (Revelation 20:10).

Messiah to Be Descended From Abraham

Genesis 22:15-18 Then *the angel of the Lord called to Abraham a second time from heaven, and said, "By Myself, I have sworn, declares the Lord, ...in your seed all the nations of the earth shall be blessed, ..."*

Mathew 1:1 *"The book of the genealogy of Yeshua the Messiah, the son of David, the son of Abraham."*

CHAPTER 2 – HOW TO IDENTIFY THE MESSIAH: A STUDY OF MESSIANIC PROPHECY

Galatians 3:16 *"Now the promises were spoken to Abraham and to his seed. He does not say, "and to seeds," as referring to many, but rather to one, "and to your seed," that is, Messiah."*

Messiah to Be Descended from Jacob

Numbers 24:17 *"I see Him, but not now; I behold Him, but not near; a star shall come forth from Jacob, and a scepter shall rise from Israel, He shall crush through the forehead of Moab, and tear down all the sons of Seth."*

Luke 3:34 *"Jesus, the son of Jacob, the son of Isaac, the son of Abraham, the son of Terah, the son of Nahor."*

Messiah to Be Descended from the Tribe of Judah

Genesis 49:10 *"The scepter shall not depart from Judah, nor the ruler's staff from between his feet, until Shiloh comes, And to Him shall be the obedience of the peoples."*

As we saw earlier, "Shiloh" is seen by both Rabbinic and Christian authorities as a reference to the Messiah. This prophecy speaks to the fact that "Shiloh" will inherit the authority of the Kingly Tribe of Judah, and the obedience of the people. Other prophecies indicate that the people here refer not only to the Jewish people but also to the nations (see Isaiah 42:6 and 49:6).

Matthew 1:1-2 *"The book of the genealogy of Yeshua the Messiah, the son of David, the son of Abraham. To Abraham was born Isaac; and to Isaac, Jacob; and to Jacob, Judah and his brothers;"*

Luke 3:33 *"Jesus.... the son of ………. Judah,"*

Messiah to Be Descended from King David

The New Testament writers are very careful to identify Yeshua's legal right to the throne of his illustrious ancestor. He is seen as the One whom the prophets identified as that primary descendant of King David who would have the eternal throne rights to rule the nation of Israel.

2 Samuel 7:12-13 *"When your days are complete, and you lie down with your fathers, I will raise up your descendant after you, who will come forth from you, and I will establish His Kingdom." He shall build a house for My name, and I will establish the throne of His Kingdom forever."*

Psalm 132:11 *"The Lord has sworn to David a truth from which He will not turn back; "Of the fruit of your body I will set upon your throne."*

Isaiah 11:1 *"There shall come forth a Rod out of the stem of Jesse, and a Branch shall grow out of his roots."*

Jeremiah 33:17 *"Thus says the Lord; David shall never lack a man to sit upon the throne of the house of Israel."*

Jeremiah 23:5-6 *"Behold, the days are coming, declares the Lord, when I shall raise up for David a Righteous Branch; He will reign as King and act wisely and do justice and righteousness in the land. In His days Judah will be saved, and Israel will dwell securely; and this is His name by which He will be called, "The Lord our Righteousness."*

Matthew 1:1 *"The book of the genealogy of Jesus Christ, the son of David, the son of Abraham."*

Luke 1:32-33 *"He will be great and will be called the Son of the Highest, and the Lord God will give Him the throne of His father David, and He will reign over the house of Jacob forever, and His Kingdom will have no end."*

CHAPTER 2 – HOW TO IDENTIFY THE MESSIAH: A STUDY OF MESSIANIC PROPHECY

Acts 2:29-30 *"Brethren, I may confidently say to you regarding the patriarch David that he both died and was buried, and his tomb is with us to this day. And so, because he was a prophet, and knew that God had sworn to him with an oath to seat one of his descendants upon his throne,"*

Romans 1:3 *"...concerning His Son, who was born of a descendant of David according to the flesh,"*

Messiah to Rule Israel As the Greater King David

Genesis 49:10 *"The scepter shall not depart from Judah, nor the ruler's staff from between his feet, until Shiloh comes, and to Him shall be the obedience of the peoples."*

Jeremiah 30:9 *"'But they shall serve the Lord their God, and David their King, whom I will raise up for them."*

Ezekiel 34:23-24 *"Then I will set over them one shepherd, My servant David, and He will feed them; He will feed them Himself and be their Shepherd. I, the Lord, will be their God, and My servant David will be prince among them; I, the Lord, have spoken."*

Ezekiel 37:24-25 *"My servant David will be King over them, and they will all have one shepherd, and they will walk in My ordinances, and keep My statutes, and observe them. They shall live on the land that I gave to Jacob My servant, in which your fathers lived; and they will live on it, they, and their sons, and their sons' sons, forever; and David My servant shall be their prince forever."*

As you study what the Bible teaches about the One who is going to execute Judgment and Justice, you will see that the Scriptures point to this eternal King who is coming to rule the earth.

Studying Messianic prophecy is like taking a "road" through the Scriptures. No matter which "road" you choose, no matter what aspect of Messianic prophecy you study, they will all ultimately lead to the

Messiah Yeshua/Jesus. It is as He said, *"Behold, I come; in the Scroll of the Book it is written of Me"* (Psalm 40:7; Luke 24:44).

CHAPTER 3 – MESSIAH'S MINISTRY

As you read through the following Scriptures consider the ways in which they depict this particular individual. Please don't let any religious or traditional bias cause you to prejudge these verses. God uses these verses to make us prayerfully ask the question, *"Of Whom Do the Prophets Speak?"*

Is there any other person throughout history, other than Yeshua/Jesus, who fits these descriptions?

Messiah Was to Have A Forerunner; A Messenger Sent to Clear the Way for the Lord

The New Testament writers recognized that the ministry of "Yochanan the Immerser" (commonly known as "John the Baptist) was the fulfillment of Isaiah's prophecy.

Isaiah 40:3 *"...a voice is crying in the wilderness, prepare ye the way of the Lord."*

Malachi 3:1 *"Behold, I am going to send My messenger, and he will clear the way before Me..."*

Matthew 3:1-3 *"Now in those days John the Baptist came, preaching in the wilderness of Judea, saying, "Repent, for the Kingdom of Heaven is at hand." For this is the one referred to by Isaiah the prophet, saying, "The voice of one crying in the wilderness, 'Make ready the way of the Lord, Make His paths straight!"*

Luke 1:17 *"It is he who will go as a forerunner before Him in the spirit and power of Elijah, to turn the hearts of the fathers back to the children, and the disobedient to the attitude of the righteous; to make ready a people prepared for the Lord."*

Messiah Was to Have a Special Anointing of the Holy Spirit

No one in the history of the world had the anointing of the Holy Spirit upon them like Yeshua did! The evidence of that were the amazing miracles that were manifested throughout His ministry. Now would be a good time to ask the Lord to manifest His Love, Power and Presence in your life. If you, or a loved one are sick, why don't you ask the Messiah to demonstrate His reality, by healing that illness.

Psalm 45:7 *"You have loved righteousness, and hated wickedness; Therefore God, Your God, has anointed You with the Oil of Joy above your fellows."*

Isaiah 11:1-5 *"Then a shoot will spring from the stem of Jesse, and a branch from His roots will bear fruit. The Spirit of the Lord will rest on Him, the spirit of wisdom and understanding, the spirit of counsel and strength, the spirit of knowledge and the fear of the Lord. He will delight in the fear of the Lord, and He will not judge by what His eyes see, nor make a decision by what His ears hear; But with righteousness He will judge the poor, and decide with fairness for the afflicted of the earth; and He will strike the earth with the rod of His mouth, and with the breath of His lips He will slay the wicked. Also, righteousness will be the belt about His loins, and faithfulness the belt about His waist."*

Isaiah 42:6-7 *"I am the Lord, I have called you in righteousness, I will also hold you by the hand and watch over you, I will appoint you as a Covenant to the people, as a light to the nations, to open blind eyes, to bring out prisoners from the dungeon, and those who dwell in darkness from the prison.*

Isaiah 61:1 *"The Spirit of the Lord God is upon Me Because the Lord has anointed Me to bring Good News to the afflicted; He has sent Me to bind up the brokenhearted, to proclaim liberty to captives, and freedom to prisoners;"*

Matthew 3:16-17 *"After being baptized, Jesus went up immediately from the water; and behold, the Heavens were opened, and he saw the Spirit of God descending as a dove, and coming upon Him, and behold, a voice out of the Heavens, saying, "This is My Beloved Son, in whom I am well-pleased."*

Matthew 11:4-6 *"Jesus answered and said to them, "Go and report to John what you hear and see: the blind receive sight and the lame walk, the lepers are cleansed, and the deaf hear, and the dead are raised up, and the poor have the Gospel preached to them. Blessed is he who keeps from stumbling over Me."*

Luke 4:18-21 *"The Spirit of the Lord is upon Me because He anointed Me to preach the Gospel to the poor. He has sent Me to proclaim release to the captives, and recovery of sight to the blind, to set free those who are downtrodden, to proclaim the favorable year of the Lord. He closed the book, and gave it back to the attendant, and sat down, and the eyes of all in the synagogue were fixed upon Him. He began to say to them, "Today this Scripture has been fulfilled in your hearing."*

John 3:35-36 *"The Father loves the Son and has given all things into His hand. He who believes in the Son has eternal life, but he who does not obey the Son shall not see life, but the wrath of God abides on him."*

John 11:47 *"Therefore the chief priests and the Pharisees convened a council, and were saying, "What are we doing? For this man is performing many signs."*

Messiah to Pour Out the Holy Spirit

As you read these verses you can ask the Lord to pour His Spirit upon you also!

Joel 2:28-29 *"It will come about after this that I will pour out My Spirit on all mankind, and your sons and daughters will prophesy, your old men will dream dreams, your young men will see visions. And even on the male and female servants, I will pour out My Spirit in those days."*

John the Immerser said this in Matthew 3:11 *"As for me, I baptize you with water for repentance, but He who is coming after me is mightier than I, and I am not fit to remove His sandals; He will baptize you with the Holy Spirit and fire."*

Acts 2:16-18 *"This is what was spoken of through the prophet Joel: "And it shall be in the last days, God says, "I will pour forth of My Spirit upon all mankind; your sons and your daughters shall prophesy, your young men shall see visions, and your old men shall dream dreams; Even upon My servants, both men and women, I will in those days pour forth of My Spirit, and they shall prophesy."*

Galilee to Be an Area of Messiah's Ministry

Isaiah 9:1-2 *"... the land of Zebulun and the land of Naphtali...He shall make glorious, by the way of the sea, on the other side of Jordan, Galilee of the Gentiles. The people who walk in darkness will see a great light; those who live in a dark land, the light will shine on them."*

Matthew 4:12-16 *"... He came and settled in Capernaum, which is by the sea, in the region of Zebulun and Naphtali. This was to fulfill what was spoken through Isaiah the prophet, saying, "The land of Zebulun and the land of Naphtali, By the way of the sea, beyond the Jordan, Galilee of the Gentiles, the people who were sitting in darkness saw a great light, and to those who were sitting in the land and shadow of death, upon them a light dawned."*

Messiah Will Be Very Humble and Gentle

My dear Jewish friend, have you ever read the New Testament? What do you think of the person portrayed as the Messiah there?

Isaiah 42:2-3 *"He will not cry out or raise His voice, nor make His voice heard in the street. A bruised reed He will not break, and a dimly burning wick He will not extinguish; He will faithfully bring forth justice."*

CHAPTER 3 – MESSIAH'S MINISTRY

Matthew 12:18-20 *"Behold, My servant whom I have chosen; My beloved in whom My soul is well-pleased; I will put My Spirit upon Him, and He shall proclaim justice to the Gentiles. He will not quarrel, nor cry out; nor will anyone hear His voice in the streets. A battered reed He will not break off, and a smoldering wick He will not put out until He leads justice to victory."*

Messiah Was to Teach in Parables

Psalm 78:2 *"I will open My mouth in a parable: I will utter dark sayings of old."*

Matthew 13:34-35 *"All these things Jesus spoke to the multitudes in parables, and He did not speak to them without a parable, so that what was spoken through the prophet might be fulfilled, saying, "I will open My mouth in parables; <u>I will utter things hidden since the foundation of the world.</u>"*

Messiah to Inaugurate the New Covenant and Establish a New Relationship with God for Everyone Who Believes

God promises the Jewish people a New Covenant that is not like the Covenant He made at Mt. Sinai. In the New Covenant He promises to give us a new relationship with Himself. He removes our sins, gives us a new heart, and a divinely inspired desire to obey Him.

Please do not make the mistake of dismissing the truth of the Scriptures because you see the failings of people. God's truths are not dependent on the obedience or disobedience of anyone. They stand as a spiritual "Rock" you can rely upon. There is a New Covenant you can enter, there is a new relationship with God you can enjoy. As you read these verses, ask God to make Himself and these promises real to you.

Jeremiah 31:31-34 *"Behold, days are coming, declares the Lord, when I will make a New Covenant with the house of Israel and with the house of Judah, not like the Covenant which I made with their fathers in the day I took them by the hand to bring them out of the land of Egypt, My Covenant which they broke, although I was a husband to them, declares the Lord. But this is the Covenant which I will make with the house of Israel after those days, declares the Lord, I will put My law within them, and on their heart, I will write it, and I will be their God, and they shall be My people. They shall not teach again, each man his neighbor and each man his brother, saying, 'Know the Lord,' for they shall all know me, from the least of them to the greatest of them, declares the Lord, for I will forgive their iniquity, and their sin I will remember no more."*

Ezekiel 36:24-28 *"For I will take you from the nations, gather you from all the lands, and bring you into your own land. Then I will sprinkle clean water on you, and you will be clean; I will cleanse you from all your filthiness and from all your idols. Moreover, I will give you a new heart and put a new spirit within you; and I will remove the heart of stone from your flesh and give you a heart of flesh. And I will put My Spirit within you and cause you to walk in My statutes, and you will be careful to observe My ordinances. And you will live in the land that I gave to your forefathers; so you will be My people, and I will be your God."*

Jesus personalized the prophecies of the New Covenant. He declared that He was the mediator of the New Covenant.

Luke 22:20 *"And in the same way He (Jesus) took the cup after they had eaten, saying, "This cup which is poured out for you is the New Covenant in My blood."*

1 Corinthians 11:25 *"In the same way He (Jesus) took the cup also, after supper, saying, "This cup is the New Covenant in My blood; do this, as often as you drink it, in remembrance of Me."*

The New Testament book of Hebrews was written specifically to Jewish believers in Yeshua. Here are two verses from this important book.

Hebrews 9:14-15 *"How much more will the blood of the Messiah, who through the eternal Spirit offered Himself without blemish to God,*

CHAPTER 3 – MESSIAH'S MINISTRY

cleanse your conscience from dead works to serve the living God? And for this reason, He is the mediator of a New Covenant, in order that since a death has taken place for the redemption of the transgressions that were committed under the First Covenant, those who have been called may receive the promise of the eternal inheritance."

Hebrews 12:24 *"...Jesus, the mediator of a New Covenant..."*

Jesus explained that we enter New Covenant spiritual realities by being "Born of the Spirit." This spiritual re-birth takes place when we repent of our sins and receive the Messiah into our heart, into our spirit. He forgives us, and His supernatural life is "birthed" – "imparted" into us. A simple prayer in your own words asking the Messiah to forgive you and to enter your life will open the door for your spiritual rebirth and your entrance into the Kingdom of God.

John 1:12-13 *"But as many as received Him, to them He gave the right to become children of God, even to those who believe in His name, who were born not of blood, nor of the will of the flesh, nor of the will of man, but of God."*

John 3:3-8 *"<u>Jesus answered and said to him, "Truly, truly, I say to you, unless one is Born Again he cannot see the Kingdom of God."</u> Nicodemus said to Him, "How can a man be born when he is old? He cannot enter a second time into his mother's womb and be born, can he?" Jesus answered, "Truly, truly, I say to you, unless one is born of Water and the Spirit he cannot enter into the Kingdom of God. "<u>That which is born of the flesh is flesh, and that which is Born of the Spirit is spirit. Do not be amazed that I said to you, 'You must be Born Again.'</u> "The wind blows where it wishes, and you hear the sound of it, but do not know where it comes from and where it is going; so is everyone who is Born of the Spirit."*

1 Peter 1:3, 23 *"Blessed be the God and Father of our Lord Yeshua the Messiah, who according to His great mercy has caused us to be Born Again to a living hope through the resurrection of Messiah Yeshua from the dead. For you have been Born Again not of seed*

which is perishable but imperishable, that is, through the living and abiding Word of God."

Colossians 1:13-14 *"For He rescued us from the domain of darkness and transferred us to the Kingdom of His Beloved Son, in whom we have redemption, the forgiveness of sins."*

Messiah Will Be the Redeemer of the Gentiles and a Light to the Nations

It is very interesting to consider the fact that there are people who believe in the Jewish Rabbi Yeshua in every nation. Is there any other Jew who even comes close to that? Is there any other Jew who even comes close to fulfilling these prophecies?

Isaiah 11:10 *"Then it will come about in that day that the nations will resort to the root of Jesse, who will stand as a signal for the peoples; And His resting place will be glorious."*

Isaiah 42:1 *"Behold, My Servant, whom I uphold; My chosen one in whom My soul delights. I have put My Spirit upon Him; He will bring forth justice to the nations."*

Isaiah 42:6-7 *"I the Lord have called You in righteousness, and will hold your hand, and will keep You, and give You for a Covenant of the people, for a light of the Gentiles. To open blind eyes, to bring out prisoners from the dungeon, and those who dwell in darkness from the prison."*

Isaiah 49:6 *"It is too small a thing that you should be My Servant to raise up the tribes of Jacob, and to restore the preserved ones of Israel; I will also make you a Light of the Nations so that My salvation may reach to the end of the earth."*

Matthew 12:18 *"Behold, My Servant whom I have chosen; My Beloved in whom My soul is well-pleased; I will put My Spirit upon Him, and He shall proclaim justice to the Gentiles."*

CHAPTER 3 – MESSIAH'S MINISTRY

Matthew 12:21 *"...and in His name the Gentiles will hope."*

Matthew 28:18-20 *"And Jesus came up and spoke to them, saying, "All authority has been given to Me in heaven and on earth. "Go therefore and make disciples of all the nations, baptizing them in the name of the Father and the Son and the Holy Spirit, teaching them to observe all that I commanded you; and lo, I am with you always, even to the end of the age."*

Acts 10:45 *"All the circumcised believers who had come with Peter were amazed because the gift of the Holy Spirit had been poured out upon the Gentiles also."*

Acts 13:47 *"...I have placed you as a light for the Gentiles, that you should bring salvation to the end of the earth."*

Romans 15:8-12 *"For I say that Messiah has become a servant to the circumcision on behalf of the truth of God to confirm the promises given to the fathers, and for the Gentiles to glorify God for His mercy; as it is written, "Therefore I will give praise to Thee among the Gentiles, And I will sing to Thy name." And again, He says, "Rejoice, O Gentiles, with His people." And again, "Praise the Lord all you Gentiles, and let all the peoples praise Him." And again, Isaiah says, "There shall come the root of Jesse, And He who arises to rule over the Gentiles, In Him shall the Gentiles hope."*

Galatians 3:14 *"... in Messiah Jesus the blessing of Abraham comes to the Gentiles so that we might receive the promise of the Spirit through faith."*

Messiah Will Defeat Death Itself

Isaiah 25:8 *"He will swallow up death for all time, And the Lord God will wipe tears away from all faces, and He will remove the reproach of His people from all the earth; For the Lord has spoken."*

1 Corinthians 15:54 *"But when this perishable will have put on the imperishable, and this mortal will have put on immortality, then will*

come about the saying that is written, "Death is swallowed up in Victory!"

2 Timothy 1:10 *"... that has now has been revealed by the appearing of our Savior Messiah Jesus, who abolished death, and brought life and immortality to light through the Gospel."*

Revelation 21:4 *"He shall wipe away every tear from their eyes; and there shall no longer be any death; there shall no longer be any mourning, or crying, or pain; the first things have passed away."*

CHAPTER 4 – TWO ADVENTS OF ONE MESSIAH FORETOLD BY THE PROPHETS

Allow me to repeat what I wrote earlier. Daniel 7:13 prophesies the King's coming in two different ways. The Rabbis saw this duality and created the concept of two Messiahs. One, the suffering Messiah whom they call Messiah Ben (son of) Joseph, and two, Messiah Ben David, the Messianic King who will sit on the throne of David ruling the nations. They taught that if the Jewish people are meritorious, the King will come on the Clouds of Heaven; if they are not, He will come lowly riding upon a donkey. The first time He came as the lowly suffering servant of Isaiah 53 to atone for sin. But He's coming again! This time with the Clouds of Heaven to rule and reign as King over all the earth!

As you read what the Prophets have written, you will see that the Messiah in his first coming was to minister under the anointing of the Holy Spirit and open the Kingdom of God to anyone who believed in Him. He would suffer rejection from his own people, die as an atonement for sin, rise from the dead, establish a New Covenant and become a *Light to the Nations*. Do you know of anyone other than Yeshua, Jesus, who comes anywhere remotely close to fulfilling these prophecies? If not Him, who are the Prophets speaking about?

The Messiah Would Appear First as a Suffering Servant and Then Return as a Reigning King

The Suffering Servant comes from Bethlehem, riding on a donkey.

Micah 5:2 *"But as for you, Bethlehem Ephratah, too little to be among the clans of Judah, from you One will go forth for me to be Ruler of Israel. His goings forth are from long ago, from the days of eternity."*

Zechariah 9:9 *"Rejoice greatly, O daughter of the Lord! Shout in triumph, O daughter of Jerusalem! Behold, your King is coming to you; He is just and endowed with salvation, humble, and mounted on a donkey, Even on a colt, the foal of a donkey."*

The Reigning King comes from Heaven, riding the Clouds.

Daniel 7:13-14 *"I kept looking in the night visions, and behold, with the Clouds of Heaven one like a Son of Man was coming, and He came up to the Ancient of Days and was presented before Him. And to Him was given Dominion, Glory and a Kingdom, that all the peoples, nations, and men of every language might serve Him. His Dominion is an Everlasting Dominion which will not pass away, and His Kingdom is one which will not be destroyed."*

THE PURPOSE OF HIS FIRST COMING

Messiah to minister under the Anointing of the Holy Spirit

Isaiah 11:1-3 *"Then a shoot will spring from the stem of Jesse, and a branch from His roots will bear fruit. The Spirit of the Lord will rest on Him, The Spirit of wisdom and understanding, the Spirit of counsel and strength, the Spirit of knowledge and the fear of the Lord. He will delight in the fear of the Lord, and He will not judge by what His eyes see, nor make a decision by what His ears hear;"*

Isaiah 61:1-2 *"The Spirit of the Lord is upon Me, Because the Lord has anointed Me to bring Good News to the afflicted; He has sent Me to bind up the brokenhearted, to proclaim liberty to captives, and freedom to prisoners; To proclaim the favorable year of the Lord, and the day of vengeance of our Lord; to comfort all who mourn,"*

Messiah to be a "Light to the Nations" bringing God's Salvation to the world

Isaiah 42:5-7 *"Thus says God the Lord, Who created the heavens and stretched them out, Who spread out the earth and its offspring, Who gives breath to the people on it, and spirit to those who walk in it, "I*

CHAPTER 4 – TWO ADVENTS OF ONE MESSIAH FORETOLD BY THE PROPHETS

am the Lord, I have called you in righteousness, I will also hold you by the hand and watch over you, and I will appoint you as a covenant to the people, As a Light to the Nations, to open blind eyes, to bring out prisoners from the dungeon, and those who dwell in darkness from the prison."

Isaiah 49:6 *"He says, "It is too small a thing that you should be My Servant to raise up the tribes of Jacob, and to restore the preserved ones of Israel; I will also make You a Light of the Nations so that My salvation may reach to the end of the earth."*

Messiah to die as an Atonement for Sin

Isaiah 53:7-8 *"He was oppressed, and He was afflicted, yet He did not open His mouth; Like a lamb that is led to slaughter, and like a sheep that is silent before its shearers, so He did not open His mouth. By oppression and judgment He was taken away; and as for His generation, who considered that He was cut off out of the land of the living, for the transgression of My people to whom the stroke was due."*

Messiah to rise from the dead

Psalm 16:10 *"For You will not abandon My soul to Sheol; Neither will You allow your Holy One to undergo decay."*

Isaiah 53:10 *"But the Lord was pleased to crush Him, putting Him to grief; If He would render Himself as a guilt offering, He will see His offspring, He will prolong His days, and the good pleasure of the Lord will prosper in His hand."*

Messiah to establish a New Covenant

Jeremiah 31:31-34 *"Behold, days are coming, declares the Lord, when I will make a New Covenant with the house of Israel and with the house of Judah, not like the covenant which I made with their fathers in the day I took them by the hand to bring them out of the land of Egypt, My covenant which they broke, although I was a husband to them, declares the Lord. But this is the covenant which I will make with the house of Israel after those days, declares the Lord, I will put My law within them, and on their heart, I will write it, and I will be their Lord, and they shall be My people. They shall not teach again, each man his neighbor and each man his brother, saying, 'Know the Lord,' for they shall all know Me, from the least of them to the greatest of them, declares the Lord, for I will forgive their iniquity, and their sin I will remember no more."*

THE SECOND COMING OF THE MESSIAH

As we read what the Prophets wrote, we see that Israel's Messiah and King will fulfill these prophetic promises. He will rule Israel as their Shepherd and King. He will judge the nations, rule over them, and because He is God, will receive worship from all people in every country. Not only that, because He is God, His reign shall be eternal!

THE PURPOSE OF HIS SECOND COMING IS TO:

1) Rule as Israel's Shepherd & King

Isaiah 40:9-11 *"Get yourself up on a high mountain, O Lord, bearer of good news, lift up your voice mightily, O Jerusalem, bearer of Good News; Lift it up, do not fear. Say to the cities of Judah, "Here is your Lord!" Behold, the Lord God will come with might, with His arm ruling for Him. Behold, His reward is with Him, and His recompense before Him. Like a shepherd He will tend His flock, In His arm He will gather the lambs, and carry them in His bosom; He will gently lead the nursing ewes."*

Jeremiah 23:5-6 *"Behold, the days are coming, declares the Lord, "When I shall raise up for David a righteous Branch; He will reign as King and act wisely and do justice and righteousness in the land. In His days Judah will be saved, and Israel will dwell securely; and*

CHAPTER 4 – TWO ADVENTS OF ONE MESSIAH FORETOLD BY THE PROPHETS

this is His name by which He will be called, "The Lord our Righteousness."

Ezekiel 34:23-24 *"Then I will set over them One Shepherd, My servant David, and He will feed them; He will feed them Himself and be their Shepherd. I, the Lord, will be their Lord, and My servant David will be Prince among them; I, the Lord, have spoken."*

Ezekiel 37:24-28 *"My servant David will be King over them, and they will all have One Shepherd, and they will walk in My ordinances, and keep My statutes, and observe them. They shall live on the land that I gave to Jacob My servant, in which your fathers lived; and they will live on it, they, and their sons, and their sons' sons, forever; and David My servant shall be their Prince forever. I will make a Covenant of Peace with them; it will be an Everlasting Covenant with them. I will place them and multiply them and will set My sanctuary in their midst forever. My dwelling place also will be with them, and I will be their Lord, and they will be My people. The nations will know that I am the Lord who sanctifies Israel when My sanctuary is in their midst forever."*

2) Judge the Nations

Psalm 96:13 *"The Lord is coming; For He is coming to judge the earth. He will judge the world in righteousness, and the peoples in His faithfulness."*

Psalm 98:9 *"The Lord is coming to judge the earth; He will judge the world with righteousness, and the peoples with equity."*

Isaiah 11:4-5 *"But with righteousness, He will judge the poor, and decide with fairness for the afflicted of the earth; He will strike the earth with the rod of His mouth, and with the breath of His lips He will slay the wicked. Also, righteousness will be the belt about His loins, and faithfulness the belt about His waist."*

Isaiah 66:16 *"For the Lord will execute judgment by fire and by His sword on all flesh, and those slain by the Lord will be many."*

1 Chronicles 16:33 *"Then the trees of the forest will sing for joy before the Lord; For He is coming to judge the earth."*

3) Rule over all the Nations

Psalm 2:8-9 *"Ask of me, and I will surely give the nations as Your inheritance, and the very ends of the earth as Your possession. 'You shalt break them with a rod of iron; You shalt shatter them like earthenware."*

Psalm 110:5-6 *"The Lord is at your right hand; He will shatter kings in the day of His wrath. He will judge among the nations; He will fill them with corpses, He will shatter the chief men over a broad country."*

Micah 4:3 *"He will judge between many peoples and render decisions for mighty, distant nations. Then they will hammer their Swords into Plowshares and their Spears into Pruning hooks; Nation will not lift up sword against nation, and never again will they train for war."*

Isaiah 2:4 *"He will judge between the nations and will render decisions for many peoples, and they will hammer their Swords into Plowshares and their Spears into Pruning Hooks. Nation will not lift up sword against nation, and never again will they learn war."*

Isaiah 11:10 *"Then it will come about in that day that the nations will seek the Root of Jesse, who will stand as a Signal for the peoples; and His resting place will be Glorious."*

Zechariah 9:10 *"He will speak Peace to the nations; His Dominion will be from Sea to Sea, and from the River to the ends of the Earth."*

Zechariah 14:9 *"The Lord will be King over all the Earth; in that day the Lord will be the only One, and His name the only One."*

CHAPTER 4 – TWO ADVENTS OF ONE MESSIAH FORETOLD BY THE PROPHETS

4) Receive the Worship from all the Nations

Isaiah 66:23 *"...and it shall be from New Moon to New Moon and from Sabbath to Sabbath, all mankind will come to bow down before Me, says the Lord."*

Zechariah 8:22-23 *"So many peoples and mighty nations will come to seek the Lord of Hosts in Jerusalem and to entreat the favor of the Lord. Thus says the Lord of Hosts, 'In those days ten men from all the nations will grasp the garment of a Jew saying, "Let us go with you, for we have heard that the Lord is with you."*

Zechariah 14:16-18 *"Then it will come about that any who are left of all the nations that went against Jerusalem will go up from year to year to worship the King, the Lord of Hosts, and to celebrate the Feast of Booths. It will be that whichever of the families of the earth does not go up to Jerusalem to worship the King, the Lord of Hosts, there will be no rain on them. If the family of Egypt does not go up or enter, then no rain will fall on them; it will be the plague with which the Lord smites the nations who do not go up to celebrate the Feast of Booths."*

5) His Reign Shall Be Eternal

Daniel 2:44 *"In the days of those kings the Lord of Heaven will set up a Kingdom which will never be destroyed, and that Kingdom will not be left for another people; it will crush and put an end to all these kingdoms, but it will itself endure forever."*

Daniel 7:13-14 *"I kept looking in the night visions, and behold, with the clouds of Heaven One like a Son of Man was coming, and He came up to the Ancient of Days and was presented before Him. To Him was given Dominion, Glory and a Kingdom that all the peoples, nations, and men of every language might serve Him. His Dominion is an Everlasting Dominion which will not pass away, and His Kingdom is one which will not be destroyed."*

Isaiah 9:6-7 *"For a child will be born to us, a son will be given to us, and the government will rest on His shoulders; and His name will be called Wonderful Counselor, Mighty God, Eternal Father, Prince of Peace. There will be no end to the increase of His government or peace, on the throne of David and over His Kingdom, to establish it and to uphold it with justice and righteousness from then on and forevermore. The zeal of the Lord of Hosts will accomplish this."*

Psalm 145:13 *"Your Kingdom is an everlasting Kingdom, and Your Dominion endures throughout all generations."*

Revelation 19:11-16 *"And I saw heaven opened, and behold a white horse, and He who sat upon it is called Faithful and True; and in righteousness, He judges and wages war. And His eyes are a flame of fire, and upon His head are many diadems, and He has a name written upon Him which no one knows except Himself. And He is clothed with a robe dipped in blood, and His name is called The Word of God. And the armies which are in heaven, clothed in fine linen, white and clean, were following Him on white horses. And from His mouth comes a sharp sword, so that with it He may smite the nations; and He will rule them with a rod of iron; and He treads the winepress of the fierce wrath of God, the Almighty. And on His robe and on His thigh, He has a name written, "KING OF KINGS, AND LORD OF LORDS."*

CHAPTER 5 – THE MESSIAH: A PROPHET, A PRIEST, AND A KING

The Necessity of a Prophet, Priest, and King

Deuteronomy 18:15-16 - We need a Prophet to speak to us because of sin's darkness; therefore, God established a *Prophetic order*.

Leviticus chapters 1-7 - We need a Priest to intercede and offer atoning sacrifices for us because of sin's guilt; therefore, God established a *Sacrificial system*.

2 Samuel 7:16; Zechariah 14:9-21 - We need a King to rule over us because of sin's lawlessness; therefore, God inaugurated a *Kingly line*.

The Prophet

A Unique Prophet Like Moses Will Come

As we will see in chapter 6, there are amazing parallels between the life of Moses and Jesus.

In Deuteronomy 18:15-19 we read of God's promise to raise up another prophet just like Moses.

"The Lord your God will raise up for you a prophet like me from among you, from your countrymen, you shall listen to Him…and I will put My words in His mouth, and He shall speak to them all that I command Him. It shall come about that whoever will not listen to My words which He shall speak in My name, I Myself will require it of him."

The New Testament recognizes that Yeshua is that Prophet.

John 6:14 *"When therefore the people saw the sign which He had performed, they said, "This is of a truth the Prophet who is to come into the world."*

John 7:40 *"Some of the multitude, therefore, when they heard these words, were saying, "This certainly is the Prophet."*

Acts 3:19-26 *"Repent therefore and return, that your sins may be wiped away, in order that times of refreshing may come from the presence of the Lord; and that He may send Jesus, the Christ appointed for you, whom heaven must receive until the period of restoration of all things about which God spoke by the mouth of His holy prophets from ancient time. "Moses said, 'The Lord God shall raise up for you a prophet like me from your brethren; to Him, you shall give heed to everything He says to you. 'And it shall be that every soul that does not heed that prophet shall be utterly destroyed from among the people.' "And likewise, all the prophets who have spoken, from Samuel and his successors onward, also announced these days. "It is you who are the sons of the prophets, and of the covenant which God made with your fathers, saying to Abraham, 'And in your seed, all the families of the earth shall be blessed.' "For you first, God raised up His Servant, and sent Him to bless you by turning every one of you from your wicked ways."*

THE PRIEST

The Levitical Priests Offered Atoning Sacrifices for Israel

Leviticus 4:26, 31, 35
[26] *"And all its fat he shall offer up in smoke on the altar as in the case of the fat of the sacrifice of peace offerings. Thus the priest shall make atonement for him regarding his sin, and he shall be forgiven."*

[31] *"Then he shall remove all its fat, just as the fat was removed from the sacrifice of peace offerings; and the priest shall offer it up in smoke on the altar for a soothing aroma to the Lord. Thus, the priest shall make atonement for him, and he shall be forgiven."*

CHAPTER 5 – THE MESSIAH: A PROPHET, A PRIEST, AND A KING

35 "Then he shall remove all its fat, just as the fat of the lamb is removed from the sacrifice of the peace offerings, and the priest shall offer them up in smoke on the altar, on the offerings by fire to the Lord. Thus, the priest shall make atonement for him regarding his sin which he has committed, and he shall be forgiven."

Leviticus 5:6, 10, 13, 16, 18
6 "He shall also bring his guilt offering to the Lord for his sin which he has committed, a female from the flock, a lamb or a goat as a sin offering. So, the priest shall make atonement on his behalf for his sin."

10 "The second he shall then prepare as a burnt offering according to the ordinance. So, the priest shall make atonement on his behalf for his sin which he has committed, and it shall be forgiven him."

13 "So the priest shall make atonement for him concerning his sin which he has committed from one of these, and it shall be forgiven him; then the rest shall become the priest's, like the grain offering."

16 "And he shall make restitution for that which he has sinned against the holy thing and shall add to it a fifth part of it and give it to the priest. The priest shall then make atonement for him with the ram of the guilt offering, and it shall be forgiven him."

18 "He is then to bring the priest a ram without defect from the flock, according to your valuation, for a guilt offering. So, the priest shall make atonement for him concerning his error in which he sinned unintentionally and did not know it, and it shall be forgiven him."

Messiah Will Be a Priest After the Order of Melchizedek

God revealed that another order of Priesthood would be established. It would be modeled after the Priesthood of Melchizedek who is introduced to us in Genesis 14:18-19. Melchizedek was both the *"King of Salem,"* and a *"Priest of God Most High"* who blessed Abraham after serving him bread and wine. It is interesting to note that Yeshua used the "bread and wine" of the Passover Seder to symbolically represent His *"broken body and shed blood"* which would atone for sin and be the foundation of the New Covenant (Luke 22:19-20).

Psalm 110:4 *The Lord has sworn and will not change His mind, "You are a Priest forever according to the order of Melchizedek."*

Hebrews 2:17 *Therefore, He had to be made like His brethren in all things, that He might become a merciful and faithful High Priest in things pertaining to God, to make propitiation for the sins of the people."*

Hebrews 5:6 *"You are a Priest forever according to the order of Melchizedek."*

Hebrews 6:20 *"Jesus ... become a High Priest forever according to the order of Melchizedek."*

Hebrews 7:17 *"Thou art a Priest forever according to the order of Melchizedek."*

Hebrews 9:11-12 *"But when Messiah appeared as a High Priest of the good things to come, He entered through the greater and more perfect Tabernacle, not made with hands, that is to say, not of this creation; and not through the blood of goats and calves, but through His own Blood, He entered the Holy Place once for all, having obtained eternal redemption."*

Hebrews 10:12 *"But He, after He had offered one sacrifice for sins forever, sat down on the right hand of God."*

As a Priest, Yeshua Is Now Interceding for Us

Romans 8:34 *"Messiah Jesus is He who died, yes, rather who was raised, who is at the right hand of God, who also intercedes for us."*

Hebrews 7:25 *"He is able to save forever those who draw near to God through Him since He always lives to make intercession for them."*

THE KING

David's Seed Will Be King Forever

Psalm 89:3-4, 29 *"I have made a Covenant with My chosen; I have sworn to David, My servant, I will establish your seed forever and build up Your throne to all generations.... I will establish His descendants forever and His throne as the days of Heaven."*

Jesus Is That King

Luke 1:32-33 *"He shall be great and shall be called the Son of the Highest: and the Lord God shall give unto Him the throne of His father David: and He shall reign over the house of Jacob forever, and of His Kingdom, there shall be no end."*

He Was Born as a King

Matthew 2:2 *"...Where is He that is born King of the Jews? We have seen His star in the east and have come to worship Him."*

He Was Crucified as a King

John 19:19 *"Pilate wrote an inscription also and put it on the cross. And it was written, "Jesus the Nazarene, the King of the Jews."*

Many in Israel Recognized That He Was Their King

John 12:12-15 *"On the next day the great multitude who had come to the Feast, when they heard that Jesus was coming to Jerusalem, took the branches of the palm trees, and went out to meet Him, and began* to cry out, "Hosanna! Blessed is He who comes in the name of the Lord, even the King of Israel." And Jesus, finding a young donkey, sat on it; as it is written, "Fear not, daughter of Zion; behold, your King is coming, seated on a donkey's colt."

This was the fulfillment of Zechariah 9:9 *"Rejoice greatly, O daughter of Zion! Shout in triumph, O daughter of Jerusalem! Behold, your King is coming to you; He is just and endowed with salvation, Humble, and mounted on a donkey, Even on a colt, the foal of a donkey."*

Jesus Declared That He Was the King of Israel

John 18: 37 *"Therefore Pilate said to Him, "So You are a King?" Jesus answered, "You say correctly that I am a King. For this, I have been born, and for this I have come into the world, to testify to the truth. Everyone who is of the truth hears My voice."*

As King He Shall Return in Power and Glory

Matthew 16:27 *"For the Son of Man is going to come in the glory of His Father with His angels and will then recompense every man according to his deeds."*

Matthew 24:30 *"... then the sign of the Son of Man will appear in the sky, and then all the tribes of the earth will mourn, and they will see the Son of Man coming on the clouds of the sky with power and great glory."*

Matthew 25:31 *"But when the Son of Man comes in His glory, and all the angels with Him, then He will sit on His glorious throne."*

1 Thessalonians 4:16 *"For the Lord Himself will descend from Heaven with a shout, with the voice of the archangel, and with the trumpet of God; and the dead in Messiah shall rise first."*

Jude 1:14 *"Behold, the Lord is coming with many thousands of His Holy Ones, to execute judgment upon all…"*

Revelation 19:11-16 *"I saw Heaven opened, and behold a white horse, and He who sat upon it is called Faithful and True, and in righteousness, He judges and wages war. His eyes are a flame of fire, and upon His head are many diadems, and He has a name written upon Him which no one knows except Himself. He is clothed with a robe dipped in blood, and His name is called The Word of God. The armies which are in Heaven, clothed in fine linen, white and clean, were following Him on white horses. From His mouth comes a sharp sword, so that with it He may smite the nations; and He will rule them with a rod of iron; and He treads the winepress of the fierce wrath of God, the Almighty. On His robe and on His thigh He has a name written, "King of Kings, and Lord of Lords."*

The Messianic King Will Rule Over the Nations

Psalm 2:6-9 *"But as for Me, I have installed My King Upon Zion, My holy mountain. I will surely tell of the decree of the Lord: He said to Me, 'You are My Son, Today I have begotten Thee. Ask of Me, and I will surely give the nations as Your inheritance, and the very ends of the earth as Your possession. You shalt break them with a rod of iron; You shalt shatter them like earthenware."*

Daniel 7:13-14 *"I saw in the night visions and, behold, one like the Son of man came with the clouds of Heaven and came to the Ancient of days, and they brought Him near before Him. There was given Him dominion, and glory, and a Kingdom, that all people, nations, and languages, should serve Him: His dominion is an everlasting dominion, which shall not pass away, and His Kingdom that which shall not be destroyed."*

Isaiah 2:4 *"He will judge between the nations and will render decisions for many peoples; they will hammer their swords into plowshares, and their spears into pruning hooks. Nation will not lift up sword against nation, and never again will they learn war."*

Jeremiah 23:5-6 *"Behold, the days come, says the Lord, that I will raise unto David a righteous Branch and a King shall reign and prosper, and shall execute judgment and justice in the earth. In His days Judah shall be saved, and Israel shall dwell safely; and this is His name whereby He shall be called, The Lord our Righteousness."*

Micah 4:1-4 *"And it will come about in the last days that the mountain of the house of the Lord will be established as the chief of the mountains. It will be raised above the hills, and the peoples will stream to it. And many nations will come and say, "Come and let us go up to the mountain of the Lord and to the house of the God of Jacob, that He may teach us about His ways and that we may walk in His paths. For from Zion will go forth the law, even the word of the Lord from Jerusalem. And He will judge between many peoples and render decisions for mighty, distant nations. Then they will hammer their swords into plowshares and their spears into pruning hooks; Nation will not lift up sword against nation, and never again will they train for war. And each of them will sit under his vine and under his fig tree, with no one to make them afraid, for the mouth of the Lord of Hosts has spoken."*

CHAPTER 6 – CONSIDER THESE AMAZING PARALLELS BETWEEN THE LIFE OF MOSES AND JESUS

As Infants, Their Lives Were Sought by Evil Tyrants.

Moses
Exodus 1:22 *"Then Pharaoh commanded all his (Hebrew) people, saying, "Every son who is born you are to cast into the Nile, and every daughter you are to keep alive."*

Jesus
Matthew 2:16-17 *"Then when Herod saw that he had been tricked by the Magi, he became very enraged, and sent and slew all the male children who were in Bethlehem and in all its environs, from two years old and under, according to the time which he had ascertained from the Magi."*

Their Parents Hid Them from Certain Death.

Moses
Exodus 2:3-10 *"But when she could hide him no longer, she got him a wicker basket and covered it over with tar and pitch. Then she put the child into it and set it among the reeds by the bank of the Nile. And his sister stood at a distance to find out what would happen to him. Then the daughter of Pharaoh came down to bathe at the Nile, with her maidens walking alongside the Nile; and she saw the basket among the reeds and sent her maid, and she brought it to her. When she opened it, she saw the child, and behold; the boy was crying. And she pitied him and said, "This is one of the Hebrews' children." Then his sister said to Pharaoh's daughter, "Shall I go and call a nurse for you from the Hebrew women, that she may nurse the child for you?" And Pharaoh's daughter said to her, "Go ahead." So, the girl went and called the child's mother. Then Pharaoh's daughter said to her, "Take this child away and nurse him for me and I shall give you your wages." So, the woman took the child and nursed him. And the child*

grew, and she brought him to Pharaoh's daughter, and he became her son. And she named him Moses, and said, "Because I drew him out of the water."

Jesus
Matthew 2:13-15 *"Now when they had departed, behold, an angel of the Lord appeared to Joseph in a dream, saying, "Arise and take the Child and His mother, and flee to Egypt, and remain there until I tell you; for Herod is going to search for the Child to destroy Him. And he arose and took the Child and His mother by night and departed for Egypt; and was there until the death of Herod, that what was spoken by the Lord through the prophet might be fulfilled, saying, "Out of Egypt did I call My Son."*

Both Were Sent from God.

Moses
Exodus 3:10 *"Therefore, come now, and I will send you to Pharaoh, so that you may bring My people, the sons of Israel, out of Egypt."*

Jesus
John 8:42 *"Jesus said, "If God were your Father, you would love Me; for I proceeded forth and have come from God, for I have not even come on My own initiative, but He sent Me."*

Supernatural Signs Confirmed the Callings of Moses and Jesus.

Moses
Exodus 4:5-9 *"that they may believe that the Lord, the God of their fathers, the God of Abraham, the God of Isaac, and the God of Jacob, has appeared to you."* [6] *And the Lord furthermore said to him, "Now put your hand into your bosom." So, he put his hand into his bosom, and when he took it out, behold, his hand was leprous like snow.* [7] *Then He said, "Put your hand into your bosom again." So, he put his hand into his bosom again; and when he took it out of his bosom, behold, it was restored like the rest of his flesh.* [8] *"And it shall come*

CHAPTER 6 – CONSIDER THESE AMAZING PARALLELS BETWEEN THE LIFE OF MOSES AND JESUS

about that if they will not believe you or heed the witness of the first sign, they may believe the witness of the last sign. [9] *"But it shall be that if they will not believe even these two signs or heed what you say, then you shall take some water from the Nile and pour it on the dry ground; and the water which you take from the Nile will become blood on the dry ground."*

Jesus
Matthew 3:16-4:1 *"And after being baptized, Jesus went up immediately from the water; and behold, the heavens were opened, and he saw the Spirit of God descending as a dove, and coming upon Him, and behold, a voice out of the heavens, saying, "This is My Beloved Son, in whom I am well-pleased."*

Both Had a Special Intimacy with God.

Moses
Exodus 33:11 *"Thus the Lord used to speak to Moses face to face, just as a man speaks to his friend. When Moses returned to the camp, his servant Joshua, the son of Nun, a young man, would not depart from the tent."*

Exodus 33:20-23 *"But He said, "You cannot see My face, for no man can see Me and live!" Then the Lord said, "Behold, there is a place by Me, and you shall stand there on the rock; and it will come about, while My glory is passing by, that I will put you in the cleft of the rock and cover you with My hand until I have passed by. "Then I will take My hand away, and you shall see My back, but My face shall not be seen."*

Deuteronomy 34:10 *"Since then no prophet has risen in Israel like Moses, whom the Lord knew face to face."*

Numbers 12:6-8 *"Hear now My words: If there is a prophet among you, I, the Lord, shall make Myself known to him in a vision. I shall speak with him in a dream. Not so, with My servant Moses, He is faithful in all My household; With him, I speak mouth to mouth, even openly, and not in dark sayings, and he beholds the form of the Lord."*

Jesus

John 1:1 *"In the beginning was the Word, and the Word was with God, and the Word was God."*

John 5:20 *"For the Father loves the Son and shows Him all things that He Himself is doing; and greater works than these will He show Him, that you may marvel."*

Matthew 17:3-5 *"And behold, Moses and Elijah appeared to them, talking with Him. And Peter answered and said to Jesus, "Lord, it is good for us to be here; if You wish, I will make three tabernacles here, one for You, and one for Moses, and one for Elijah." While he was still speaking, behold, a bright cloud overshadowed them; and behold, a voice out of the cloud, saying, "This is My Beloved Son, with whom I am well-pleased; listen to Him!"*

John 14:9-11 *"Jesus said to him, "Have I been so long with you, and yet you have not come to know Me, Philip? He who has seen Me has seen the Father; how do you say, 'Show us the Father'? Do you not believe that I am in the Father, and the Father is in Me? The words that I say to you I do not speak on My own initiative, but the Father abiding in Me does His works. Believe Me that I am in the Father, and the Father in Me; otherwise believe because of the works themselves."*

Both Are Unique Prophets.

Moses

Deuteronomy 18:18-19 *"I will raise up a prophet from among their countrymen like you, and I will put My words in his mouth, and he shall speak to them all that I command him. 'And it shall come about that whoever will not listen to My words which he shall speak in My name, I Myself will require it of him."*

Deuteronomy 34:10 *"Since then no prophet has risen in Israel like Moses, whom the Lord knew face to face."*

CHAPTER 6 – CONSIDER THESE AMAZING PARALLELS BETWEEN THE LIFE OF MOSES AND JESUS

Jesus
Matthew 17:5 *"While he was still speaking, behold, a bright cloud overshadowed them; and behold, a voice out of the cloud, saying, "This is My beloved Son, with whom I am well-pleased; listen to Him!"*

John 6:14 *"When therefore the people saw the sign which He had performed, they said, "This is of a truth the Prophet who is to come into the world."*

John 12:48-50 *"He who rejects Me, and does not receive My sayings, has one who judges him; the word I spoke is what will judge him on the last day. For I did not speak on My own initiative, but the Father Himself who sent Me has given Me commandment, what to say, and what to speak. And I know that His commandment is eternal life; therefore the things I speak, I speak just as the Father has told Me."*

Hebrews 1:1-2 *"God, after He spoke long ago to the fathers in the prophets in many portions and in many ways, in these last days has spoken to us in His Son, whom He appointed heir of all things, through whom also He made the world."*

Both Are Intercessors.

Moses
Exodus 20:18-21 *"And all the people perceived the thunder and the lightning flashes and the sound of the trumpet and the mountain smoking; and when the people saw it, they trembled and stood at a distance. Then they said to Moses, "Speak to us yourself and we will listen; but let not God speak to us, lest we die." And Moses said to the people, "Do not be afraid; for God has come to test you, and so that the fear of Him may remain with you, so that you may not sin." So, the people stood at a distance, while Moses approached the thick cloud where God was."*

Exodus 32:11-14 *"Then Moses entreated the Lord his God, and said, "O Lord, why does your anger burn against your people whom you have brought out from the land of Egypt with great power and with a mighty hand? "Why should the Egyptians speak, saying, 'With evil intent He brought them out to kill them in the mountains and to destroy them from the face of the earth'? Turn from your burning anger and change your mind about harming your people. "Remember Abraham, Isaac, and Israel, your servants to whom you did swear by yourself, and did say to them, 'I will multiply your descendants as the stars of the heavens, and all this land of which I have spoken I will give to your descendants, and they shall inherit it forever.'" So, the Lord changed His mind about the harm which He said He would do to His people."*

Jesus
Isaiah 53:12 *"Therefore, I will give Him a portion with the great, And He will divide the booty with the strong; Because He poured out Himself to death and was numbered with the transgressors, yet He Himself bore the sin of many and interceded for the transgressors."*

John 17:9 *"I ask on their behalf; I do not ask on behalf of the world, but of those who You have given Me; for they are yours."*

John 17:20 *"I do not ask on behalf of these alone, but for those also who believe in Me through their word."*

Hebrews 7:24-25 *"He, on the other hand, because He abides forever, holds His priesthood permanently. Hence, also, He is able to save forever those who draw near to God through Him, since He always lives to make intercession for them."*

Both Are Inaugurators of a Divine Covenant.

Moses
Exodus 19:7-9 *"So Moses came and called the elders of the people and set before them all these words which the Lord had commanded him. And all the people answered together and said, "All that the Lord has spoken we will do!" And Moses brought back the words of the people to the Lord. And the Lord said to Moses, "Behold, I shall come to you in a thick cloud, so that the people may hear when I speak with you and may also believe in you forever."*

CHAPTER 6 – CONSIDER THESE AMAZING PARALLELS BETWEEN THE LIFE OF MOSES AND JESUS

Exodus 24:6-8 *"And Moses took half of the blood and put it in basins, and the other half of the blood he sprinkled on the altar. Then he took the Book of the Covenant and read it in the hearing of the people; and they said, "All that the Lord has spoken we will do, and we will be obedient!" So, Moses took the blood and sprinkled it on the people, and said, "Behold the Blood of the Covenant, which the Lord has made with you in accordance with all these words."*

Deuteronomy 5:2-5 *"The Lord our God made a Covenant with us at Horeb. The Lord did not make this Covenant with our fathers, but with us, with all those of us alive here today. The Lord spoke to you face to face at the mountain from the midst of the fire, while I was standing between the Lord and you at that time, to declare to you the Word of the Lord; for you were afraid because of the fire and did not go up the mountain."*

Jesus
Hebrews 8:6-7 *"But now He has obtained a more excellent ministry, by as much as He is also the mediator of a better Covenant, which has been enacted on better promises. For if that first Covenant had been faultless, there would have been no occasion sought for a second."*

Hebrews 12:22-24 *"But you have come to Mount Zion and to the city of the living God, the heavenly Jerusalem, and to myriads of angels, to the general assembly and church of the first-born who are enrolled in heaven, and to God, the Judge of all, and to the spirits of righteous men made perfect, and to Jesus, the mediator of a New Covenant, and to the sprinkled Blood, which speaks better than the Blood of Abel."*

Matthew 26:28 *"...this is My blood of the Covenant, which is poured out for many for the forgiveness of sins."*

CHAPTER 7 – EVENTS OF MESSIAH'S BETRAYAL, DEATH, BURIAL, RESURRECTION, AND ASCENSION FORETOLD

As you read through this next section consider how these various Scriptures are connected to the life of Yeshua. Are all these mere "coincidences?" I believe that there is a divine thread being woven into a prophetic picture that reveals who Yeshua really is. As you see all of these "threads" please ask the Lord, *"Of Whom Do the Prophets Speak?"*

Messiah Was to Enter Jerusalem on a Donkey Bringing Salvation

Zechariah 9:9 *"Rejoice greatly, O daughter of Zion! Shout in triumph, O daughter of Jerusalem! Behold, your King is coming to you; He is just and endowed with salvation, humble, and mounted on a donkey, even on a colt, the foal of a donkey."*

Matthew 21:1-11 *"When they had approached Jerusalem and had come to Bethphage, to the Mount of Olives, then Jesus sent two disciples, saying to them, "Go into the village opposite you, and immediately you will find a donkey tied there and a colt with her; untie them, and bring them to me. If anyone says something to you, you shall say, 'The Lord has need of them,' and immediately he will send them." Now, this took place that what was spoken through the prophet might be fulfilled, saying, "Say to the daughter of Zion, 'Behold your King is coming to you, gentle, and mounted on a donkey, even on a colt, the foal of a beast of burden."*

The disciples went and did just as Jesus had directed them, and brought the donkey and the colt, and laid on them their garments, on which He sat. Most of the multitude spread their garments in the road, and others were cutting branches from the trees, and spreading them in the road. The multitudes going before Him, and those who followed were crying out, saying, "Hosanna to the Son of David; Blessed is He who comes in the name of the Lord; Hosanna in the highest!" When He had entered Jerusalem, all the city was stirred, saying, "Who is this?" And the multitudes were saying, "This is the prophet, Jesus, from Nazareth in Galilee."

"The King" in prophecy who comes to rule and reign is always a reference to King Messiah. Here we see the King riding on a donkey as He enters Jerusalem.

As we saw in Chapter 4, Daniel 7:13 prophesies the King coming in two different ways. The Rabbis saw this duality and created the concept of two Messiahs. The suffering Messiah whom they call Messiah Ben (son of) Joseph and Messiah Ben David, the Messianic King who will sit on the throne of David, ruling the nations. They taught that if the Jewish people are meritorious, the King will come on the Clouds of Heaven; if they are not, He will come lowly riding upon a donkey. The first time He came as the lowly suffering servant of Isaiah 53- to atone for sin. As surely as He came the first time, He is coming again! This time with the Clouds of Heaven to rule and reign as King over ALL the earth!

Messiah Was to Be Betrayed by a Friend

Psalm 41:9 *"Even My close friend, in whom I trusted, who ate My bread, has lifted up his heel against me."*

Matthew 26:23-24 *"He answered and said, "He who dipped his hand with me in the bowl is the one who will betray me. The Son of Man is to go, just as it is written of Him; but woe to that man by whom the Son of Man is betrayed! It would have been good for that man if he had not been born."*

John 13:18-21 *"... but it is that the Scripture may be fulfilled, "He who eats My bread has lifted up his heel against me." When Jesus had said this, He became troubled in spirit, and testified, and said, "Truly, truly, I say to you, that one of you will betray me."*

CHAPTER 7 – EVENTS OF MESSIAH'S BETRAYAL, DEATH, BURIAL, RESURRECTION, AND ASCENSION FORETOLD

Messiah Was to Be Sold for Thirty Pieces of Silver and the Money Given for a Potter's Field

Zechariah 11:12-13 *"I said to them, "If it is good in your sight, give me My wages; but if not, never mind!" So, they weighed out thirty shekels of silver as My wages. Then the Lord said to me, "Throw it to the potter, that magnificent price at which they valued me." So, I took the thirty shekels of silver and threw them to the potter in the house of the Lord."*

Matthew 26:15 *"What are you willing to give me to deliver Him up to you?" And they weighed out to him thirty pieces of silver."*

Matthew 27:5-10 *"He threw the pieces of silver into the sanctuary and departed, and he went away and hanged himself. The chief priests took the pieces of silver and said, "It is not lawful to put them into the temple treasury since it is the price of blood." They counseled together and with the money bought the Potter's Field as a burial place for strangers. For this reason, that field has been called the Field of Blood to this day. Then that which was spoken through Jeremiah the prophet was fulfilled, saying, "They took the thirty pieces of silver, the price of the one whose price had been set by the sons of Israel, and they gave them for the Potter's Field, as the Lord directed me."*

Messiah Was to Be Mocked, Struck on the Cheek, Scourged, and Spat Upon

Micah 5:1 *"...with a rod they will smite the Judge of Israel on the cheek."*

Isaiah 50:6 *"I gave My back to those who strike me, and My cheeks to those who pluck out the beard; I did not cover My face from humiliation and spitting."*

Psalm 22:7-8 *"All they that see me laugh me to scorn: they shoot out the lip, they shake the head, saying, He trusted on the Lord that He would deliver him: let Him deliver him, seeing He delighted in Him."*

Matthew 26:67-68 *"Then they spat in His face and beat Him with their fists; and others slapped Him, and said, "Prophesy to us, You Christ; who is the one who hit You?"*

Matthew 27:30, 39-44 *"And they spat on Him, and took the reed and began to beat Him on the head...Those passing by were hurling abuse at Him, wagging their heads, and saying, "You who are going to destroy the Temple and rebuild it in three days, save yourself! If you are the Son of God, come down from the cross." In the same way the chief priests also, along with the scribes and elders, were mocking Him, and saying, "He saved others; He cannot save Himself. He is the King of Israel; let Him now come down from the cross, and we shall believe in Him. He trusts in God; let Him deliver Him now if He takes pleasure in Him; for He said, 'I am the Son of God.' And the robbers also who had been crucified with Him were casting the same insult at Him."*

Mark 14:65; 15:19-20 *"And some began to spit at Him, and to blindfold Him, and to beat Him with their fists, and to say to Him, "Prophesy!" And the officers received Him with slaps in the face...they kept beating His head with a reed, and spitting at Him, and kneeling and bowing before Him. And after they had mocked Him, they took the purple off Him and put His garments on Him. And they led Him out to crucify Him."*

Luke 22:63-65 *"The men who were holding Jesus in custody were mocking Him and beating Him, and they blindfolded Him and were asking Him, saying, "Prophesy, who is the one who hit You?" They were also saying many other things against Him, blaspheming."*

Messiah Was to Have His Garments Divided, and Lots Would Be Cast for His Clothes

Psalm 22:18 *"They divide My garments among them and cast lots for My clothing."*

Matthew 27:35 *"When they had crucified Him, they divided up His garments among themselves, casting lots."*

CHAPTER 7 – EVENTS OF MESSIAH'S BETRAYAL, DEATH, BURIAL, RESURRECTION, AND ASCENSION FORETOLD

Messiah Was to Be Crucified
(i.e., His Hands and Feet Were Pierced)

Psalm 22:11-18 *"Be not far from me, for trouble is near; for there is none to help. Many bulls have surrounded Me; Strong bulls of Bashan have encircled Me. They open wide their mouth at Me, as a ravening and a roaring lion. I am poured out like water, and all My bones are out of joint; My heart is like wax; it is melted within Me. My strength is dried up like a potsherd, and My tongue cleaves to My jaws, and you lay Me in the dust of death. For dogs have surrounded Me; a band of evildoers has encompassed Me; they pierced My hands and My feet. I can count all My bones. They look, they stare at Me; they divide My garments among them, and for My clothing they cast lots."*

Zechariah 12:10 *"....and they shall look upon Me whom they have pierced, and they shall mourn for Him, as one mourns for his only son, and shall be in bitterness for Him, as one that is in bitterness for his firstborn."*

Matthew 27:35 *"And when they had crucified Him....,"*

Luke 23:33 *"And when they came to the place called The Skull, there they crucified Him ..."*

John 20:25-29 The disciple Thomas (commonly known as "Doubting Thomas") said, *"Unless I shall see in His hands the imprint of the nails and put my finger into the place of the nails, and put my hand into His side, I will not believe." And after eight days again His disciples were inside, and Thomas with them. Jesus came, the doors having been shut, and stood in their midst, and said, "Peace be with you." Then He said to Thomas, "Reach here your finger, and see My hands; and reach here your hand and put it into My side; and be not unbelieving but believing." Thomas answered and said to Him, "My Lord and My God!"*

Messiah Was to Suffer Thirst and Be Given Vinegar

Psalm 22:15 *"My strength is dried up like a potsherd; and My tongue cleaves to My jaws, and you have brought Me into the dust of death."*

Psalm 69:21 *"They also gave Me gall for My food, and for My thirst they gave Me vinegar to drink."*

Matthew 27:34 *"They gave Him wine to drink mingled with gall; and after tasting it, He was unwilling to drink."*

John 19:28-30 *"After this, Jesus, knowing that all things had already been accomplished, so that the Scripture might be fulfilled, said, "I am thirsty." A jar full of sour wine was standing there; so they put a sponge full of the sour wine upon a branch of hyssop and brought it up to His mouth. When Jesus, therefore, had received the sour wine, He said, "It is finished!" and He bowed His head, and gave up His spirit."*

Messiah Was to Die with Criminals and Be Buried with the Rich

Isaiah 53:9 *"...He made His grave with the wicked, and with the rich in His death; because He had done no violence, neither was any deceit in His mouth."*

Matthew 27:38 *"At that time two robbers were crucified with Him, one on the right and one on the left."*

Matthew 27:57-60 *"When it was evening, there came a rich man from Arimathea, named Joseph, who himself had also become a disciple of Jesus. This man went to Pilate and asked for the body of Jesus. Then Pilate ordered it to be given over to him. Joseph took the body and wrapped it in a clean linen cloth, and laid it in his new tomb, which he had hewn out in the rock; and he rolled a large stone against the entrance of the tomb and went away."*

CHAPTER 7 – EVENTS OF MESSIAH'S BETRAYAL, DEATH, BURIAL, RESURRECTION, AND ASCENSION FORETOLD

Messiah Was to Be Resurrected from the Dead

Psalm 16:10 "...*you will not leave My soul in hell; neither wilt you allow your Holy One to see corruption.*"

Isaiah 53:10 "...*it pleased the Lord to bruise Him; He has put Him to grief; when you shalt make His soul an offering for sin, He shall see His seed, He shall prolong His days, and the pleasure of the Lord shall prosper in His hand.*"

Acts 2:29-32 "*Brethren, I may confidently say to you regarding the patriarch David that he both died and was buried, and his tomb is with us to this day.* "*Because he was a prophet and knew that God had sworn to him with an oath to seat one of his descendants upon his throne, he looked ahead and spoke of the resurrection of the Messiah, that He was neither abandoned to Hades, nor did His flesh suffer decay. This Jesus God raised up again, to which we are all witnesses.*"

Acts 13:33-37 "*God has fulfilled this promise to our children in that He raised up Jesus, as it is also written in the second Psalm, 'You are My Son; today I have begotten Thee.' And as for the fact that He raised Him up from the dead, no more to return to decay, He has spoken in this way: 'I will give you the holy and sure blessings of David.' Therefore, He also says in another Psalm, 'You will not allow your Holy One to undergo decay.' For David, after he had served the purpose of God in his own generation, fell asleep, and was laid among his fathers, and underwent decay; but He whom God raised did not undergo decay.*"

Messiah Was to Ascend to Heaven

Psalm 68:18 "*You have ascended on high, you have led captivity captive.*"

Mark 16:19 "*So then, when the Lord Jesus had spoken to them, He was received up into Heaven, and sat down at the right hand of God.*"

Ephesians 4:8 *"Therefore it says, "When He ascended on high, He led captive a host of captives, and He gave gifts to men."*

Acts 1:9 *"And after He had said these things, He was lifted up while they were looking on, and a cloud received Him out of their sight."*

Acts 2:33 *"Therefore having been exalted to the right hand of God and having received from the Father the promise of the Holy Spirit, He has poured forth this which you both see and hear."*

Messiah is to Sit at the Right Hand of God

Psalm 110:1 *The Lord said unto My Lord, "Sit at My right hand until I make your enemies a footstool for Your feet."*

Matthew 26:64 *"Jesus said to him, "You have said it yourself; nevertheless, I tell you, hereafter you shall see the Son of Man sitting at the right hand of Power and coming on the Clouds of Heaven."*

Hebrews 1:3 *"He is the radiance of His glory and the exact representation of His nature and upholds all things by the word of His power. When He had made purification of sins, He sat down at the right hand of the Majesty on high."*

Ephesians 1:19-22 *"These are in accordance with the working of the strength of His might which He brought about in the Messiah, when He raised Him from the dead, and seated Him at His right hand in the Heavenly places, far above all rule and authority and power and dominion, and every name that is named, not only in this age, but also in the one to come. He put all things in subjection under His feet and gave Him as head over all things to the Church."*

1 Peter 3:22 *"Jesus the Messiah, ... who is at the right hand of God, having gone into Heaven, after angels and authorities and powers had been subjected to Him."*

CHAPTER 7 – EVENTS OF MESSIAH'S BETRAYAL, DEATH, BURIAL, RESURRECTION, AND ASCENSION FORETOLD

The Purpose of Messiah's Death Was to Atone for Sin

Daniel 9:24-25 *"Seventy weeks have been decreed for your people and your holy city, to finish the transgression, to make an end of sin, to make atonement for iniquity, to bring in everlasting righteousness, to seal up vision and prophecy and to anoint the Most Holy Place. So you are to know and discern that from the issuing of a decree to restore and rebuild Jerusalem until Messiah the Prince there will be seven weeks and sixty-two weeks."*

Isaiah 53:5 *"He was bruised for our iniquities and wounded for our transgressions."*

Matthew 26:28 *"This is My Blood of the Covenant, which is poured out for many for the forgiveness of sins."*

Act 5:31 *"He is the One whom God exalted to His right hand as a Prince and a Savior, to grant repentance to Israel and forgiveness of sins."*

1 Corinthians 15:3 *"For I delivered to you as of first importance what I also received, that Messiah died for our sins according to the Scriptures,"*

1 Peter 2:24 *"He Himself bore our sins in His body on the cross, that we might die to sin and live to righteousness; for by His wounds you were healed."*

Hebrews 9:28 *"So Messiah also, having been offered once to bear the sins of many, shall appear a second time for salvation without reference to sin, to those who eagerly await Him."*

CHAPTER 8 – MESSIAH WAS TO BE REJECTED BY THE JEWISH PEOPLE

Messiah Was to Be a Stone of Stumbling, a Rock of Offense, Yet Be the Chief Cornerstone

Psalm 118:22-23 *"The stone which the builders rejected has become the Chief Corner Stone. This is the Lord's doing; It is marvelous in our eyes."*

Isaiah 8:14 *"He shall be for a sanctuary; but for a Stone of Stumbling and a Rock of Offense to both the houses of Israel, for a trap and a snare to the inhabitants of Jerusalem."*

Isaiah 28:16 *"Therefore thus says the Lord God, Behold, I lay in Zion for a foundation a Stone, a tried Stone, a precious Corner Stone, a sure foundation: he that believes will not be disturbed."*

Matthew 21:42-46 *"Jesus said to them, "Did you never read in the Scriptures, 'The Stone which the builders rejected, this became the Chief Corner Stone; this came about from the Lord, and it is marvelous in our eyes'? "Therefore, I say to you, the Kingdom of God will be taken away from you and be given to a nation producing the fruit of it, and he who falls on this Stone will be broken to pieces; but on whomever it falls, it will scatter him like dust."*

Romans 9:31-33 *"... They stumbled over the stumbling stone," "just as it is written, "Behold, I lay in Zion a stone of stumbling and a rock of offense, and he who believes in Him will not be disappointed."*

1 Peter 2:6-8 *"For this is contained in Scripture: "Behold I lay in Zion a choice Stone, a precious Corner Stone, and he who believes in Him shall not be disappointed. This precious value, then, is for you who believe. But for those who disbelieve, the Stone which the builders rejected, this became the very Cornerstone and a Stone of stumbling and a Rock of Offense; for they stumble because they are disobedient to the Word, and to this they were also appointed."*

Other Scriptures That Declare The Messiah Would Be Rejected By His Own People

Isaiah 53:1-3 *"Who has believed our report? And to whom is the arm of the Lord revealed? For He shall grow up before Him as a tender plant, and as a root out of a dry ground: He has no form nor comeliness; and when we shall see Him, there is no beauty that we should desire Him. He is despised and rejected of men; a man of sorrows and acquainted with grief: and we hid as it were our faces from Him; He was despised, and we esteemed Him not."*

Isaiah 49:7 *"Thus says the Lord, the Redeemer of Israel, and His Holy One, to the despised One, to the One abhorred by the nation, to the servant of rulers, "Kings shall see and arise, Princes shall also bow down; Because of the Lord who is faithful, the Holy One of Israel who has chosen You."*

Zechariah 13:7 *"Awake, O sword, against My shepherd, and against the man, My associate," declares the Lord of Hosts. "Strike the Shepherd that the sheep may be scattered, and I will turn My hand against the little ones."*

Psalm 69:9 *"Zeal for your house has consumed Me, the reproaches of those who reproach You have fallen on Me."*

Micah 5:1 *"They shall smite the judge of Israel with a rod upon the cheek."*

The rejection of the Messiah by his own people is not a surprise for those who study the Bible. Isaiah chapter 53 clearly prophesied that He would be rejected. The Hebrew prophets were continually confronting Israel's rejection of God and embracing of idolatry. This is the tragic history of the nation of Israel throughout the Biblical era. Their sins eventually led to the destruction of the First and Second Temple and their exile, dispersion and suffering among the nations. This was what God said would happen to his beloved, but rebellious people (Leviticus 26:14-39 and Deuteronomy 28:15-68).

CHAPTER 8 – MESSIAH WAS TO BE REJECTED BY THE JEWISH PEOPLE

Please don't think the Jewish people are unique in their rejection of Jesus. Most of humanity is in rebellion to the God of Israel, rejecting Him, His Commandments, and His Messiah. Please read how Psalm 2 describes this.

During the Exodus, the Jewish people acted in such overt rebellion to God, and His servant Moses, that God was willing to destroy the entire nation and create a new one from the descendants of Moses. They were spared because of Moses' intercession.

Exodus 32:9-14 *"And the Lord said to Moses, "I have seen this people, and behold, they are an obstinate people. "Now then let Me alone, that My anger may burn against them, and that I may destroy them; and I will make of you a great nation." Then Moses entreated the Lord his God, and said, "O Lord, why does Your anger burn against Your people whom You have brought out from the land of Egypt with great power and with a mighty hand? "Why should the Egyptians speak, saying, 'With evil intent He brought them out to kill them in the mountains and to destroy them from the face of the earth. Turn from Thy burning anger and change Your mind about doing harm to Your people. "Remember Abraham, Isaac, and Israel, Your servants to whom You did swear by Yourself, and did say to them, 'I will multiply your descendants as the stars of the heavens, and all this land of which I have spoken I will give to your descendants, and they shall inherit it forever.'" So the Lord changed His mind about the harm which He said He would do to His people."*

This is a powerful lesson for all of us who pray for the Jewish people and for God's purposes for all of humanity. Pray the Scriptural promises and prophecies back to the Lord. Remind Him of what He has said!!

Isaiah 62:6-7 *"On your walls, O Jerusalem, I have appointed watchmen; All day and all night they will never keep silent. You who remind the Lord, take no rest for yourselves; And give Him no rest until He establishes and makes Jerusalem a praise in the earth."*

The Jewish people are unique however, because of their Eternal Covenant with God (Jeremiah 31:35-37). As God's "Chosen People," they are in a special place of responsibility, calling and purpose (Exodus 19:5-6; Deuteronomy 7:6; 14:2). Their disobedience and rebellion brought the most severe consequences and punishment (Leviticus 26:14-39 and Deuteronomy 28:15-68). But that is not the end of their story. Along with the judgments of God for their sins are also many promises of redemption and ultimate great blessings that both the Hebrew Scriptures and the New Testament promise that they will yet inherit (Leviticus 26:3-13; Deuteronomy 26:18-19; 28:1-14; Isaiah 61:6-7; 62:7-12).

In the eleventh chapter of the New Testament book of Romans we learn that Israel's rejection of Jesus as their Messiah and King was part of God's plan to redeem the world. We also learn there that the Jewish people as a nation will one day receive a revelation of who Jesus really is, repent of that rejection, and receive Him as their Messianic Redeemer and King (see also Isaiah 25:6-9; Zechariah 12:10). When that history changing revelation happens, the Apostle Paul said it would be *"life from the dead."* This teaches us that when the Jewish people receive Yeshua, He will literally return to the earth, raise the dead, and set up His Kingdom on the earth and rule the nations from Jerusalem! (see Zechariah 14:1-4; Matthew 23:39; John 5:25-29; Romans 11:15, 26; 1 Corinthians 15:51-53; 1 Thessalonians 4:14-17; 2 Thessalonians 1:7; 2 Peter 3:7; Jude 1:15).

CHAPTER 9 – THE DEITY OF THE MESSIAH

The deity of Jesus is perhaps the greatest stumbling block for Jewish people because they see this as idolatry. They accuse the "Church" of deifying a man. If the "Church" did that it would be guilty of Idolatry. But we must let the Prophets speak for themselves, and decide if they are actually declaring that God will incarnate Himself as a Man. Of course, this is not impossible for God. As we study the Scriptures we see that Messiah is human in His birth at Bethlehem, but He has existed from eternity. He is born as a human being, yet He is "God with us" who will rule the world as Israel's King.

Messiah Had an Eternal Pre-Existence

Micah 5:2 *"But as for you, Bethlehem Ephratah, too little to be among the clans of Judah, from you One will go forth for Me to be the ruler of Israel. His goings forth are from long ago, from the Days of Eternity."*

Messiah Called Mighty God and Eternal Father

Isaiah 9:6 *"For a child will be born to us, a son will be given to us, and the government will rest on His shoulders; and His name will be called Wonderful Counselor, Mighty God, Eternal Father, Prince of Peace."*

The Messianic King Who Sits on David's Throne Is Called "The Lord Our Righteousness."

Jeremiah 23:5-6 *"Behold, the days are coming," declares the Lord, "When I shall raise up for David a righteous branch; and He will reign as King and act wisely and do justice and righteousness in the land. In His days Judah will be saved, and Israel will dwell securely; and this is His name by which He will be called, 'The Lord our Righteousness.'"*

The King's Dominion Is Everlasting

Daniel 7:13-14 *"I kept looking in the night visions, and behold, with the clouds of Heaven One like a Son of Man was coming, and He came up to the Ancient of Days and was presented before Him. To Him was given dominion, Glory and a Kingdom that all the peoples, nations and men of every language might serve Him. His dominion is an everlasting dominion which will not pass away, and His Kingdom is one which will not be destroyed."*

The King Over the Whole Earth Is Called God's Son

Psalm 2:6-9 *"But as for me, I have installed My King upon Zion, My holy mountain. I will surely tell of the decree of the Lord: He said to me, 'You are My Son, today I have begotten You. Ask of Me, and I will surely give the nations as your inheritance, and the very ends of the earth as your possession. You shall break them with a rod of iron; You shall shatter them like earthenware."*

The Eternal God Has a Son - Do You Know His Name?

Proverbs 30:4 *"Who has ascended into Heaven and descended? Who has gathered the wind in His fists? Who has wrapped the waters in His garment? Who has established all the ends of the earth? What is His name or His son's name? Surely you know!"*

Isaiah 7:14 *"Therefore the Lord Himself shall give you a sign; Behold, a virgin shall conceive, and bear a son, and shall call His name Immanuel, which means "God with us."*

Isaiah 9:6 *"For unto us a child is born, unto us, a son is given: and the government shall be upon His shoulder: and His name shall be called Wonderful, Counselor, The Mighty God, The Everlasting Father, The Prince of Peace."*

Daniel 7:13-14 *"I saw in the night visions and, behold, one like the Son of Man came with the Clouds of Heaven and came to the Ancient of days, and they brought Him near before Him. There was given Him Dominion, and glory, and a Kingdom, that all people, nations, and languages, should serve Him: His Dominion is an everlasting Dominion, which shall not pass away, and His Kingdom that which shall not be destroyed."*

Zechariah 14:9 *"The Lord shall be King over all the earth: in that day there shall be One Lord and His Name One."*

What kind of a PERSON can be from old, from everlasting?
How can a CHILD be called Mighty God, Everlasting Father?
Does God have a SON?

The Tri-Unity of God

I prefer to use the word "tri-unity" than "Trinity" to hopefully clarify the issue of the triune nature of the God of Israel. As we study the Hebrew Scriptures, we can see that there is a plurality of persons in the Godhead. If the idea of a triune God is not Jewish, then neither is the Hebrew Bible!

Consider this verse carefully. Here the Creator, who identifies Himself as "the First and the Last," testifies that the "Lord God and His Spirit" has sent Him.

Isaiah 48:12-16 *"Listen to Me, O Jacob, even Israel whom I called; I am He, I am the first, I am also the last. Surely My hand founded the earth, and My right hand spread out the Heavens; when I call to them, they stand together. Assemble, all of you, and listen! Who among them has declared these things? The Lord loves Him; He will carry out His good pleasure on Babylon, and His arm will be against the Chaldeans. I, even I, have spoken; indeed I have called Him, I have brought Him, and He will make His ways successful. Come near to Me, listen to this: From the first I have not spoken in secret, from the time it took place, I was there. And now the Lord God has sent Me, and His Spirit."*

A Plural God

Genesis 1:26   God said, *"Let us make man in our image, according to our likeness."*

Genesis 3:22   God said, *"They have become like one of us, knowing good and evil."*

Genesis 11:7   God said, *"Come, let us go down and there confuse their language ...."*

Isaiah 6:8   God said, *"...who will go for us?"*

Deuteronomy 6:4 The famous Jewish declaration of faith, called the Shema ("Hear!"), begins with these words:

"Shema Yisrael, Adonai Elohenu, Adonai Echad"
"Hear O Israel, the Lord our God, the Lord is One."

The Jewish people are taught that this verse means that God exists as an absolute individual. The revered Rabbi Maimonides (also known as the Rambam) of the Middle Ages, in his *Thirteen Articles of Faith*, which is the basis for much of Rabbinic theology, replaced the Hebrew word "Echad," which appears in the Bible and means a unity of more than one component, with another word, "Yachid," that means an absolute "one" or singular individual. Maimonides influenced the Jewish people so greatly that they accepted his erroneous teaching that God is a "Yachid." However, the word for "one" in the Shema is the Hebrew word "Echad," which means "a composite unity," i.e., "out of many, one."

Here are some other examples of how "Echad" is used:

Genesis 2:24 - *"...a man shall leave his father and his mother, and be joined to his wife, and they shall become one (Echad) flesh."* Two become One.

CHAPTER 9 – THE DEITY OF THE MESSIAH

Numbers 13:23 - *Then they came to the valley of Eshkol and from there cut down a branch with a single (Echad) cluster of grapes".* The cluster of many is referred to as One.

Ezekiel 37:17 – *"Then join them for yourself one (Echad) to another into one (Echad) stick that they may become one (Echad) in your hand."*
Two sticks become One.

Two Lords

Genesis 19:24 *"The Lord (hwhy) rained brimstone and fire on Sodom and Gomorrah, from the Lord (hwhy) out of the Heaven."*

[One "Jehovah" on earth calls down fire from the other "Jehovah" in Heaven! - Share this with Jehovah's Witnesses the next time they come to your door!]

"Jehovah" is a mispronunciation of the "Tetragrammaton" – the four-letter name of God in Hebrew - hwhy - and generally pronounced "Yahweh" or "Yahveh," although there is debate as to its correct pronunciation. hwhy is typically translated as "LORD" in most English versions.

Pay attention to who is speaking to whom in the following verses:

The Lord Who Will Dwell in Zion Declares That the Lord of Hosts Has Sent Him

Zechariah 2:10-11 *"Sing for joy and be glad, O daughter of Zion; for behold I am coming, and I will dwell in your midst," declares the Lord. "Many nations will join themselves to the Lord in that day and will become My people. Then I will dwell in your midst, and you will know that the Lord of Hosts has sent Me to you."*

The Lord Sends His Messenger, Who Is the Lord!

Malachi 3:1 *"Behold, I am going to send My messenger, and He will clear the way before Me. And the Lord, whom you seek, will suddenly come to His Temple; the Messenger of the Covenant, in whom you delight, behold, He is coming," says the Lord of Hosts."*

God Anoints God with the Oil of Gladness

Psalm 45:6-7 *"Your throne, O God, is forever and ever; a scepter of uprightness is the scepter of your Kingdom. You have loved righteousness and hated wickedness; Therefore, God, Your God, has anointed You with the oil of joy above your fellows."*

David's Son Is His Lord

Psalm 110:1 *"The Lord says to My Lord: "Sit at My right hand until I make your enemies a footstool for Your feet."*

Matthew 22:41-46 *"Now while the Pharisees were gathered together, Jesus asked them a question: "What do you think about the Messiah, whose son is He?" They said to Him, "The son of David." He said to them, "Then how does David in the Spirit call Him 'Lord,' saying, 'The Lord said to My Lord, "Sit at My right hand until I put your enemies beneath Your feet"'? "If David then calls Him 'Lord,' how is He His Son?" No one was able to answer Him a word, nor did anyone dare from that day on to ask Him another question."*

A Third Divine Person: The Holy Spirit

These are only a few of the references to the Holy Spirit in the Hebrew Scriptures.

CHAPTER 9 – THE DEITY OF THE MESSIAH

Genesis 1:2 *"The Spirit of God was moving over the surface of the waters."*

Genesis 6:3 *"My Spirit shall not strive . . ."*

Job 33:4 *"The Spirit of the Lord has made me."*

Psalm 51:11 *"Do not take your Holy Spirit from me."*

Isaiah 11:2 *"The Spirit of the Lord shall rest upon Him."*

Isaiah 63:10, 11 *"But they rebelled and grieved His Holy Spirit."* *"He put His Holy Spirit in the midst of them."*

Psalm 139:7 *"Where can I flee from Your Spirit?"*

Here is a list of verses from the New Testament that show that the Holy Spirit has the attributes of a person and is referred to with the personal pronoun "He." The Holy Spirit is not an "it." He is not simply a "force" or a "divine influence."

He testifies about Jesus	John 15.26
He is called the Helper	John 16:7; Acts 9:31
He convicts the world of sin	John 16:8
He guides into all truth	John 16.13; Acts 8.37
He glorifies Jesus	John 16:14
He empowers	Acts 1:8
He testifies	Romans 8:16
He helps us in prayer	Romans 8:5, 26
He searches & reveals	Romans 11:33-34; 1 Corinthians 2:10-11
He can be grieved	Ephesians 4:30

The Angel of the Lord

Consider also a very special person mentioned many times in the Hebrew Scriptures. He is called "The Angel of the Lord." In almost every passage where He is found, He is referred to as both the Angel of the Lord and the Lord Himself. In Exodus 23:20-23, this Angel is said to have the power to forgive sins, because God's name is in Him, and so He must be obeyed without question. Remember that only God can forgive sins; see Isaiah 43:25; Psalm 130:4.

Exodus 23:20-23 *"Behold, I am going to send an angel before you to guard you along the way, and to bring you into the place which I have prepared. "Be on your guard before him and obey his voice; do not be rebellious toward him, for he will not pardon your transgression since My name is in him. "But if you will truly obey his voice and do all that I say, then I will be an enemy to your enemies and an adversary to your adversaries. "For My angel will go before you and bring you into the land of the Amorites, the Hittites, the Perizzites, the Canaanites, the Hivites and the Jebusites; and I will completely destroy them."*

Compare the following verses in which the Angel is identified as God:

Compare Genesis 16:7 with Genesis 16:13
*"Now the **Angel of the Lord** found her by a spring of water in the wilderness, by the spring on the way to Shur. He said, "Hagar, Sarai's maid, where have you come from and where are you going?" She said, "I am fleeing from the presence of my mistress Sarai." Then she called the Name of the Lord who spoke to her, "**You are a God** who sees;" for she said, "Have I even remained alive here after seeing Him?"*

The Angel of the Lord, who also speaks as the Lord Himself, appears to Abraham:

*"The **Angel of the Lord** called to him from Heaven and said, "Abraham, Abraham!" He said, "Here I am." He said, "Do not stretch out your hand against the lad, and do nothing to him; for now I know that you fear God since you have not withheld your son, your only son, from Me." "Then the **Angel of the Lord** called to Abraham a second time from Heaven and said, "**By Myself,** I have sworn,*

CHAPTER 9 – THE DEITY OF THE MESSIAH

*declares **the Lord**, because you have done this thing and have not withheld your son, your only son, I will greatly bless you...."*

The Angel of the Lord, who also speaks as the Lord Himself, appears to Jacob:

Genesis 31:11 *"Then the **Angel of God** said to me in the dream, 'Jacob,' and I said, 'Here I am."*

Genesis 31:13 *"I am the **God of Bethel**, where you anointed a pillar, where you made a vow to Me; now arise, leave this land, and return to the land of your birth."*

The Angel of the Lord, who also speaks as the Lord Himself, appears to Moses:

Exodus 3:2 *"And the **Angel of the Lord** appeared to him in a blazing fire from the midst of a bush; and he looked, and behold, the bush was burning with fire, yet the bush was not consumed."*

Exodus 3:4 *"When the Lord saw that he turned aside to look, **God** called to him from the midst of the bush, and said, "Moses, Moses!" And he said, "Here I am."*

Jesus Continually Asserted His Divinity

Consider these "I AM" proclamations, and the other declarations Yeshua made about Himself

Matthew 12:8 *"...the Son of Man is Lord of the Sabbath."*

John 6:35, 41, 48 *"I am the Bread of Life."*

John 6:51 *"I am the Living Bread."*

John 6:63 *"My Words are Spirit and Life."*

John 8:12; 9:5 *"I am the Light of the World."*

John 8:51 *"Truly, truly, I say to you, if anyone keeps My word he shall never see death."*

John 8:58 *"Before Abraham was born, I am."*

John 10:7, 9 *"I am the Door of the Sheep."*

John 10:11, 14 *"I am the Good Shepherd."*

John 10:30 *"The Father and I are One."*

John 10:36 *"I am the Son of God."*

John 11:25 *"I am the Resurrection, and the Life."*

John 14:6 *"I am the Way, the Truth, and the Life."*

John 14:6 *"No one comes to the Father but through Me."*

John 15:1, 5 *"I am the True Vine."*

When Jesus made these amazing and provocative statements, He was intentionally not allowing Himself to be easily dismissed as just a good man, a great teacher or a prophet. He drew a "line in the sand." He was stating that He was, in fact, the God of Israel incarnated as a man, or He was a liar or a lunatic. There is no other choice. Each one of us must choose. Is Jesus a liar? Is He a lunatic? Or Is He Lord!

The New Testament writers declared that Jesus was "God" in many places, here is a sample:

Matthew 1:23 *"Behold, the virgin shall be with child and shall bear a Son, and they shall call His name Immanuel,"* which translated means, *"God with us."*

John 1:1 *"In the beginning was the Word, and the Word was with God, and the Word was God."*

CHAPTER 9 – THE DEITY OF THE MESSIAH

John 20:28 *"Thomas answered and said to Him, "My Lord and My God!"*

Titus 2:13 *"...looking for the blessed hope and the appearing of the glory of our great God and Savior, Messiah Jesus ...."*

Hebrews 1:8 *"But of the Son He says, "Thy throne, O God, is forever and ever...."*

2 Peter 1:1 *"Simon Peter, a bond-servant, and apostle of Jesus Christ, to those who have received a faith of the same kind as ours, by the righteousness of our God and Savior, Jesus Christ."*

In the Book of Revelation chapter 22 verse 13 (and in 1:8, 17, and 21:6) Jesus asserts His deity. He declares that He is:

> *"The Alpha and Omega, the Beginning and the End, the First and the Last"*

Compare this verse with Isaiah 41:4 - *"Who has performed and accomplished this, calling forth the generations from the beginning? I, the Lord, am the first, and with the last. I am He."*

So we see that the God of Israel's eternal nature is also attributed to the Messiah Yeshua!

CHAPTER 10 – EVIDENCE FOR THE RESURRECTION OF JESUS FROM THE DEAD

The Proclamation of The Gospel Is Built Upon The Foundation of The Resurrection of Jesus From The Dead!

Acts 1:3 *"... He presented Himself alive, after His suffering, by many convincing proofs, appearing to them over a period of forty days, and speaking of the things concerning the Kingdom of God."*

The Apostles are our witnesses that Jesus rose from the dead. What motivates their testimony? Their declaration that Jesus was alive caused them to risk everything, including the loss of their lives. Liars don't risk everything for something they know to be a lie. The Apostles proved the righteous quality of their character by their willingness to suffer and sacrifice everything, because they knew Jesus had risen from the dead and was truly the Messiah.

Were these Apostles deceived? Did they believe something that's simply not true? Did they suffer from wishful thinking and hallucinations when, as a group, they encountered the resurrected Jesus? People do not experience identical hallucinations. They were hardworking, down to earth people, who all had times of doubt and unbelief. They would not have made up such a story or simply believed it because someone told them it was so. Again, they certainly wouldn't have risked everything unless they had solid evidence.

What are the facts? Jesus died, was buried, wrapped in grave clothes and placed in a tomb. This tomb was closed with a large stone which had a seal on it. The tomb was guarded by Roman soldiers. On the third day, the tomb was empty. The stone was moved, the seal broken, and Jesus' empty grave clothes were left inside.

So, what happened to His body?

Did the disciples steal it? There is no reason for this. Why would they steal it to proclaim then He was alive and risk their lives for what they knew to be a lie? They would not.

Did the Jews steal it? They would have no motive for doing this; they wanted Him dead! If they knew where the body was, they would have produced it and ended the Apostles' preaching of Jesus' resurrection.

Did the Romans steal it? They had no reason to do this. They wanted no more trouble. The guards were charged to guard the tomb so that no one could steal the body.

Jesus escaped because he was not actually dead, but merely unconscious. However, the facts are:

- He was nearly beaten to death before the crucifixion.
- He was crucified, and his side pierced by a spear.
- The Roman executioners determined he was dead. They were professionals who knew what dead was!
- He was wrapped in grave clothes and placed in a tomb which was covered by a huge stone with a seal attached and guards to protect it.

Could He then gather enough strength in a cold, dark tomb to unwrap Himself, move a massive stone and then sneak past the guards who would not have seen or heard this huge stone move! Then where would He go? Not to His disciples. How could they then testify, at the risk of their lives, that He was resurrected, if they saw Him beaten to a pulp and half dead? If He left to hide away forever, the disciples would not have had a "Jesus is alive from the dead" message, but a "Jesus is missing" mystery. This would have left them very discouraged and disillusioned, not empowered to preach a message that was very dangerous.

We must conclude that Jesus rose from the dead!!!

His Grave Clothes Were Left Behind, and He Appeared in His Resurrected Body Many Times.

John 20:4-7 *"And the two were running together, and the other disciple ran ahead faster than Peter, and came to the tomb first; and stooping and looking in, he saw the linen wrappings lying there; but*

CHAPTER 10 – EVIDENCE FOR THE RESURRECTION OF JESUS FROM THE DEAD

he did not go in. Simon Peter therefore also came, following him, and entered the tomb; and he beheld the linen wrappings lying there, and the face-cloth, which had been on His head, not lying with the linen wrappings, but rolled up in a place by itself."

Matthew 28:9, 17 *"And behold, Jesus met them and greeted them. And they came up and took hold of His feet and worshiped Him…" And when they saw Him, they worshiped Him; but some were doubtful."*

Luke 24:36-40 *"While they were telling these things, He Himself stood in their midst. But they were startled and frightened and thought that they saw a spirit. And He said to them, "Why are you troubled, and why do doubts arise in your hearts? See My hands and My feet that it is I Myself; touch Me and see, for a spirit does not have flesh and bones as you see that I have." And when He had said this, He showed them His hands and His feet."*

Acts 1:3 *"To these He also presented Himself alive, after His suffering, by many convincing proofs, appearing to them over a period of forty days, and speaking of the things concerning the Kingdom of God."*

1 Corinthians 15:3-8 *"For I delivered to you as of first importance what I also received, that Christ died for our sins according to the Scriptures, and that He was buried, and that He was raised on the third day according to the Scriptures, and that He appeared to Cephas, then to the twelve. After that, He appeared to more than five hundred brethren at one time, most of whom remain until now, but some have fallen asleep; then He appeared to James, then to all the Apostles; and last of all, as it were to one untimely born, He appeared to me also."*

The Apostles were transformed by their encounters with the resurrected Lord. Seeing an empty tomb would not transform them. Seeing a half-dead man would not transform them. Experiencing the resurrected Messiah did transform them into the fearless miracle working apostles whose ministries changed the world!

Since that amazing day, the resurrected Lord Jesus has been transforming lives by the power of the Holy Spirit!

May God grant you boldness and love as you share with Jewish people how the Lord Jesus has changed your life.

CHAPTER 11 – ANSWERING SOME COMMON JEWISH OBJECTIONS TO JESUS

When you share your faith with Jewish people, you will probably run into these common objections to the Messiahship and Deity of Jesus. It is important that as you respond, you do it in a way that expresses the love of God. Whenever you present the Gospel, it should never be done with hostility, but with patience and respect.

It is wise to let 2 Timothy 2:24-26 be your guide:

"The Lord's bond-servant must not be quarrelsome, but be kind to all, able to teach, patient when wronged,
with gentleness correcting those who are in opposition, if perhaps God may grant them repentance leading to the knowledge of the truth...."

When you are responding to various objections, you may find that it is appropriate to agree when a good point is made. If you don't know the answer to a question or how to respond to an objection, simply admit it, and promise to study the issues further. Ask if you can continue the conversation and get their contact information. You may find that you have found a new friend.

Many objections are based on the horrific history of Christian anti-Semitism that has made Jesus the founder of a religion that hates the Jewish people. Some objections are emotionally based on Jewish cultural or traditional beliefs that reject Jesus, without ever having learned what the Bible teaches about the Messiah. Your conversation should always refer to what the Bible teaches. While we always acknowledge the sins of the Church, we must be clear that the religion of Christianity is **not** the message we are presenting.

The message is always about Yeshua, who He is and what He did. We have to stress the atonement His death, burial and resurrection provide. We have to present the opportunity for a "spiritual rebirth" and a new relationship with God that He offers. Don't let the Devil get you off track with the various objections. Keep the conversation focused on Yeshua. He is the "Author" of everyone's salvation (Hebrews 2:10).

Never allow yourself to be troubled by rejection. They are not rejecting you, but Jesus! Your job is to present who Jesus is and what He did. It's the Holy Spirit's job to bring conviction and revelation.

OBJECTION # 1: IF YOU BELIEVE IN JESUS, YOU STOP BEING JEWISH!

This is simply not true. Let us remember that Jesus was born, lived, ministered, died and was resurrected as a Jew. His genealogy is traced back to Abraham. He was an Orthodox Jew who was respected by followers and foes alike as a Rabbi. He was born in Bethlehem, raised in Nazareth and ministered only (with rare exceptions) to the Jewish people in the land of Israel.

The New Covenant Scriptures were written by Jews to proclaim and explain how Jesus is the Jewish Messiah and that He fulfilled many prophecies made by Moses and the Hebrew prophets. This includes the establishment of the New Covenant the God of Israel promised to the Jewish people (Jeremiah 31:31-34; Matthew 26:28; Luke 22:20; 1 Corinthians 11:25).

Jesus said of Himself, *"You search the Scriptures because you think that in them you have eternal life; and it is these that bear witness of Me"* (John 5:39).

In one of His post-resurrection appearances, Yeshua opened the Scriptures to two of His disciples. Luke 24:27 records it this way: *"And beginning with Moses and with all the prophets, He explained to them the things concerning Himself in all the Scriptures."*

Remember, the New Covenant Scriptures are thoroughly Jewish. They are full of quotes from the Tanach, which is another name for the Hebrew Bible. It is an acronym of the first Hebrew letter of each of the three traditional parts of the Bible: **Torah** (literally

CHAPTER 11 – ANSWERING SOME COMMON JEWISH OB-JECTIONS TO JESUS

"instructions") – specifically the first five books of Moses, **N**evi'im (from the Hebrew word for Prophet, Navi) – refers to the Prophets, and **K**etuvim (the Hebrew word for "Writings"), i.e., Job, Psalms, Proverbs, etc. Hence, TaNaKh.

All of the New Covenant's doctrines and theology, and even its thought forms are in complete harmony with everything that the Tanach reveals and teaches. All the major themes of the Hebrew Scriptures are reiterated in the New Covenant. God's Holiness, righteousness, love, forgiveness, and desire for reconciliation with those who repent, as well as man's sin, disobedience, alienation and estrangement from God are seen in both the Old and New Testament.

The offer to receive genuine faith, true hope, inner peace, great joy and unconditional love are also made available to everyone who believes.

The great themes of sacrifice and redemption, as well as warnings of judgment and promises of rewards, are clearly stated in both Testaments. Both also boldly declare the ultimate triumph of God's Kingdom on the earth (Isaiah 11:10 and Romans 15:12; Revelation 2:7 and Psalm 2; Jeremiah 31:31-37 and Hebrews 8:8-12).

The Gospel was first preached on the Jewish Holiday of Shavuot/Pentecost (Acts 2). All the original believers were Jews, of which there were many thousands. These included those who were very zealous for the Torah as well as Priests, Pharisees, and at least two that we know of, members of the Sanhedrin (Acts 2:41; 4:4; 5:14; 6:7; 21:20; John 19:37-38).

Throughout history, there have always been Jewish believers in Jesus. In fact, in the beginning it was only Jews who believed in Him. Today there are more Jewish believers in Jesus than ever before, both in Israel and around the world. At the time of this writing, there are approximately 150 Messianic congregations in Israel and hundreds around the world. It is interesting to note that the first theological controversy in the early Church was over whether Gentiles could be true followers of the Messiah without converting to Judaism since they were not Jewish (Acts 15:1-27).

There have always been Rabbis who came to faith. Isaac Lichtenstein of Hungary and Dr. Max Wertheimer were two well-known Jewish Rabbis who believed. The founder of *Chosen People Ministries* was Rabbi Leopold Cohn. When I first became a believer, I studied under a believing former Rabbi, the late Sam Stern, who founded the "Hebrew Witness" ministry in Brooklyn, New York. A search on the internet will show you other Rabbis and Jewish people from all walks of life who have come to faith in Jesus as the Messiah of Israel (See the resources section at the end of the book).

Jews Remain Jewish

Just as a Chinese, French, or English person who becomes a true Christian remains Chinese, French, or English, so a Jewish person remains Jewish! Most people believe that being a "Christian" is a cultural, family or traditional religious identity. Therefore, it is easy to understand why many Jewish people have the misconception that since Jewish parents produce Jewish babies, Christian parents produce Christian babies. What we must try to communicate is that becoming an authentic "Christian" is not a matter of physical birth but is the result of a supernatural spiritual re-birth that changes one's relationship with God, not one's "Jewishness" (John 3:3-8; 1 Peter 1:23). It is because of these facts that someone who was "born a Jew" will "die a Jew!"

Faith in the Jewish Messiah does not change one's ethnicity.

To quote an old humorous line, "Being born in a Christian home doesn't make you a Christian any more than being born in a bakery makes you a bagel." Neither Jew nor Gentile becomes a true Christian by physical birth. Christian parents do not produce Christian babies. Only the supernatural work of the Holy Spirit that reveals who Jesus is and convicts us of the need to repent and receive Him as Messiah, Lord, and Savior can produce such a spiritual re-birth. This process is accomplished by the sovereign grace of God that produces faith in Yeshua. No one can merit that grace or faith by their good works. They are free gifts that God Himself gives.

CHAPTER 11 – ANSWERING SOME COMMON JEWISH OBJECTIONS TO JESUS

Paul, the Jewish Apostle, described it this way:

> *"For by grace you have been saved through faith; and that not of yourselves, it is the gift of God; not as a result of works, that no one should boast."* (Ephesians 2:8-9)

For most Jewish people, everything about the religion of Christianity is all very "Gentile." It is outside their experience of being "Jewish" or what in some Jewish circles is called "Yiddishkeit" ("a Jewish way of life," in the Yiddish language). But we are not talking about any aspect of the modern or even historical expressions of "Gentile Christianity." We are talking about what the God of Israel has spoken through the Jewish Scriptures. After all, the message of Jesus is about the Kingdom of God, not the religion of Christianity!

Part of the confusion is how the word "Christian" is understood and used. Our Bible has been translated from Hebrew to Greek to English. As I wrote earlier, the Hebrew word for Messiah is Mashiach, (pronounced Ma-she-ach). The 'ach' part sounds like you are clearing your throat. Mashiach, which means "Anointed one" was translated to the Greek word Christos, which means "Anointed one." The Greek word Christos was then translated into the English word Christ. If the Bible had been translated directly from Hebrew to English, we would be called Messianics ("of, or belonging to, the Messiah") instead of Christians ("of, or belonging to, the Christ").

No one can become "Messianic" until they are spiritually reborn by receiving the Messiah into their heart and life. Every person, whether Jewish or Gentile, must receive the Messiah by faith to authentically become one who is "Messianic" or "Christian."

There were times when Jewish people became believers in Jesus, that Church leaders required them to renounce any allegiance to their people, religion, culture, and traditions. But the truth is that faith in Jesus requires none of that. In fact, Jewish believers often find new spiritual meaning within their historical, traditional, religious beliefs and practices. Faith in Jesus does not require that one leave their Synagogue, abandon their families or the Jewish community.

On the other hand, Jews (like myself) who come to faith in Yeshua as their Messiah have often experienced rejection by their friends and family and by the greater Jewish community. Of course, we believe this rejection is the wrong reaction. Messianic Jews regularly pose this question to our Jewish people. There are Jews who believe everything, anything, or nothing, - except that Jesus is the Messiah - but are still considered Jews. So why should one's personal belief in Jesus as the Messiah mean they are no longer considered to be a Jew, and are rejected by the Jewish world?

OBJECTION # 2: WHY DON'T THE RABBIS AND THE JEWISH PEOPLE BELIEVE?

Jewish people are brought up to not believe in Jesus. To do so is considered an act of religious and cultural *treason and betrayal*. This puts great pressure on people to not even consider the possibility that Jesus is the Messiah or to read the New Testament which is considered a non-Jewish book.

The official traditional Rabbinic rejection of Jesus goes back to the beginning of the Church in Jerusalem. It has continued with the ensuing generations of Rabbis that created and maintained their version of "Judaism," known as Rabbinic Judaism. This, combined with the Church's centuries-long horrific treatment of the Jewish people, made the complete rejection of the "founder of Christianity" a major part of Jewish self-identity.

In other words, it's this simple, Jesus is not for Jews and Jews are not for Jesus.

People are motivated by many things, often and unfortunately, the least of which is a desire to know the truth. Political, family, and financial concerns often cloud judgment and prejudice decisions. Rabbis, like all men, are fallible. The final authority for the identity of the Messiah must be the Tanach, the Jewish Bible, - not men, no matter how scholarly, religious, or pious they may be.

CHAPTER 11 – ANSWERING SOME COMMON JEWISH OB-JECTIONS TO JESUS

We must also understand that on a supernatural spiritual level the Bible teaches us that God placed a partial spiritual blindness upon Israel so that the Gospel may go to the nations.

Romans 11:1, 8, 23 *"I say then, they did not stumble so as to fall, did they? May it never be! But by their transgression salvation has come to the Gentiles, to make them jealous." ... "Just as it is written, "God gave them a spirit of stupor, eyes to see not and ears to hear not, down to this very day." ..."And they also, if they do not continue in their unbelief, will be grafted in; for God is able to graft them in again."*

Romans 11:25-26 *"For I do not want you, brethren, to be uninformed of this mystery, lest you be wise in your own estimation, that a partial hardening has happened to Israel until the fullness of the Gentiles has come in; and thus all Israel will be saved; just as it is written, "The Deliverer will come from Zion, He will remove ungodliness from Jacob."*

Jesus didn't come as the expected great political leader and heroic military conqueror, but rather as a humble servant, to atone for sins. Also, as we saw earlier, it was prophesied that He would be rejected by His people.

Zechariah 9:9 *"Rejoice greatly, O daughter of Zion; shout, O daughter of Jerusalem: behold, your King cometh unto you: He is just, and having salvation; lowly, and riding upon an ass, and upon a colt the foal of an ass."*

Isaiah 53:3-5 *"He is despised and rejected of men; a man of sorrows, and acquainted with grief: and we hid as it were our faces from Him; He was despised, and we esteemed Him not. Surely, He has borne our griefs and carried our sorrows: yet we did esteem Him stricken, smitten of God, and afflicted. But He was wounded for our transgressions; He was bruised for our iniquities: the chastisement of our peace was upon Him, and with His stripes, we are healed."*

God's Prophets were rejected (here are only two verses, there are many, many more)

Jeremiah 7:25-28 *"Since the day that your fathers came out of the land of Egypt until this day, I have sent you all My servants the prophets, daily rising early and sending them. Yet they did not listen to Me or incline their ear but stiffened their neck...."*

Jeremiah 25:4-7 *"The Lord has sent to you all His servants the prophets again and again, but you have not listened nor inclined your ear to hear...yet you have not listened to me,"*

God Himself was rejected, and, tragically, still is rejected by so many Jewish people

1 Samuel 8:7-8 *"The Lord said to Samuel, "Listen to the voice of the people regarding all that they say to you, for they have not rejected you, but they have rejected Me from being King over them. Like all the deeds which they have done since the day that I brought them up from Egypt even to this day - in that they have forsaken Me and served other gods - so they are doing to you also."*

Throughout history, there has always been a believing minority known as "The Remnant."

Isaiah 10:20-22 *"Now it will come about in that day that the remnant of Israel, and those of the house of Jacob who have escaped, will never again rely on the one who struck them, but will truly rely on the Lord the Holy One of Israel. A remnant will return, the remnant of Jacob, to the mighty God. For though your people, O Israel, are like the sand of the sea, only a remnant within them will return; a destruction is determined, overflowing with righteousness."*

1 Kings 19:10, 18 *"... I have been very jealous for the Lord God of Hosts: for the children of Israel have forsaken Your covenant, thrown down Your altars, and slain Your prophets with the sword; and I, even I only, am left; and they seek my life, to take it away" .... The Lord says, "Yet I will leave 7,000 in Israel, all the knees that have not bowed to Baal and every mouth that has not kissed him."*

Isaiah 1:9 *"Except the Lord of Hosts had left unto us a very small remnant, we should have been as Sodom, and we should have been like unto Gomorrah."*

CHAPTER 11 – ANSWERING SOME COMMON JEWISH OBJECTIONS TO JESUS

Remember, many Protestant and Catholic leaders and their followers do not believe that Jesus is the divine Son of God or believe that He is the only way of salvation. They have never been "born again." They are merely practitioners of their inherited or adopted religious traditions.

It Takes a Revelation from God to Believe in Jesus for Jews and Gentiles.

John 6:44-45, 65 *"No one can come to Me unless the Father who sent Me draws him, and I will raise him up on the last day. It is written in the prophets, 'And they shall all be taught of God.' Everyone who has heard and learned from the Father, comes to Me" .... "For this reason, I have said to you, that no one can come to me unless it has been granted him by the Father."*

Matthew 16:17 *"And Jesus answered and said to him, "Blessed are you, Simon Bar-Jonah, because flesh and blood did not reveal this to you, but My Father who is in Heaven."*

Isaiah 53:1-2 *"Who has believed our message? And to whom has the Arm of the Lord been revealed? For He grew up before Him like a tender shoot, and like a root out of parched ground; He has no stately form or majesty that we should look upon Him, nor appearance that we should be attracted to Him."*

1 Corinthians 1:30-31 *"But by His doing you are in Christ Jesus, who became to us wisdom from God, and righteousness and sanctification, and redemption...,"*

Ephesians 2:8 *"For by grace you have been saved through faith; and that not of yourselves, it is the gift of God...."*

OBJECTION # 3: IF JESUS IS THE MESSIAH, WHY DIDN'T HE BRING PEACE TO THE WORLD?

The Scriptures speak of two advents of the Messiah. He came the first time to make atonement for sin by his death and resurrection. He does impart personal inner peace to those who believe in Him and receive the forgiveness of their sins by faith in His sacrificial death and resurrection. When Jesus returns to the earth as the Messianic King, He will institute a time of global peace that will be the result of His rulership over all the earth.

As I wrote earlier, the Rabbis saw this duality and created the concept of two Messiahs. The suffering Messiah whom they call Messiah Ben (son of) Joseph and Messiah Ben David, the Messianic King who will sit on the throne of David ruling the nations.

Isaiah 7:14 *"Therefore the Lord Himself will give you a sign: Behold, a virgin will be with child and bear a son, and she will call His name Immanuel* (God with us).*"*

Micah 5:2 *"But as for you, Bethlehem Ephratah, too little to be among the clans of Judah, from you One will go forth for Me to be the ruler of Israel. His goings forth are from long ago, from the Days of Eternity."*

Isaiah 9:6 *"For a child will be born to us, a son will be given to us, And the government will rest on His shoulders; And His name will be called Wonderful Counselor, Mighty God, Eternal Father, Prince of Peace."*

Zechariah 12:10 *"I will pour upon the house of David, and upon the inhabitants of Jerusalem, the spirit of grace and of supplications: and they shall look upon Me whom they have pierced, and they shall mourn for Him, as one mourns for his only son, and shall be in bitterness for Him, as one that is in bitterness for his firstborn."*

Messiah's atoning suffering is seen in Isaiah 53 and Psalm 22.
Messiah's rulership over the nations is seen in Isaiah 11 and Psalm 2.

CHAPTER 11 – ANSWERING SOME COMMON JEWISH OB-JECTIONS TO JESUS

OBJECTION # 4: I AM A GOOD PERSON, I AM NOT A SINNER

The Jewish Bible teaches that all people are sinners in need of atonement and forgiveness. Our human standards of "goodness" are not the standards God uses to determine righteousness. His standards are His Commandments. When we break those Commandments, we become transgressors, i.e., sinners. The New Covenant revelation of the atoning death and resurrection of the Messiah presents us with an opportunity. If we open our heart to receive His sacrifice as our atonement, we can receive the amazing gift of forgiveness that God offers us. Furthermore, the New Covenant Scriptures teach that we become "righteous" before God by faith in Jesus (Romans 3:21-22; Philippians 3:9; 2 Corinthians 5:21; Ephesians 2:8-9). As evidence of that faith, we are called to live a life of "good works" (James 2:14-24).

Genesis 6:5 *"Then the Lord saw that the wickedness of man was great on the earth and that every intent of the thoughts of his heart was only evil continually."*

Genesis 8:21 *"... for the imagination of man's heart is evil from his youth...."*

Psalm 7:14 *"God is angry with sinners every day."*

Psalm 14:1-3 *"The fool has said in his heart, "There is no God." They are corrupt; they have committed abominable deeds; There is no one who does good. The Lord has looked down from Heaven upon the sons of men, to see if there are any who understand, who seek after God. They have all turned aside; together they have become corrupt; there is no one who does good, not even one."*

Psalm 53:3 *"Every one of them is gone back: they are altogether become filthy; there is none that doeth good, no, not one."*

Psalm 143:2 *"And do not enter into judgment with Thy servant, for in Thy sight no man living is righteous."*

Ecclesiastes 7:20 *"For there is not a just man upon earth, that does good and does not sin."*

Isaiah 59:2 *"But your iniquities have made a separation between you and your God, and your sins have hidden His face from you so that He does not hear."*

Isaiah 64:6 *"For all of us have become like one who is unclean, and all our righteous deeds are like a filthy garment, and all of us wither like a leaf, and our iniquities, like the wind, take us away."*

Isaiah 53:6 *".... the Lord has laid on him the iniquity of us all."*

Jeremiah 17:9 *"The heart is deceitful above all things, and desperately wicked: who can know it?"*

Ezekiel 18:3 *"Behold, all souls are mine; as the soul of the father, so also the soul of the son is mine: the soul that sins it shall die."*

OBJECTION # 5: I DON'T NEED A MEDIATOR; I CAN APPROACH GOD DIRECTLY

The Jewish people have a history of their need for a mediator and a priesthood that functions on their behalf.

Moses Interceded for the Jewish People

Exodus 20:19 *"Then they said to Moses, "Speak to us yourself and we will listen; but let not God speak to us, lest we die."*

Exodus 32:30-32 *"And it came about on the next day that Moses said to the people, "You yourselves have committed a great sin; and now I am going up to the Lord, perhaps I can make atonement for your sin." Then Moses returned to the Lord, and said, "Alas, this people has committed a great sin, and they have made a god of gold for themselves. But now, if You will, forgive their sin - and if not, please blot me out from Your Book which You have written!"*

Deuteronomy 9:25-26 *"So I fell down before the Lord the forty days and nights, which I did because the Lord had said He would destroy you. And I prayed to the Lord, and said, 'O Lord God, do not destroy Your people, even Thine inheritance, whom You have redeemed through Your greatness, whom You have brought out of Egypt with a mighty hand."*

Psalm 106:23 *"Therefore He said that He would destroy them, had not Moses His chosen one stood in the breach before Him, to turn away His wrath from destroying them."* (See also Numbers 16:44-48)

Phinehas the Priest Interceded for the People

Numbers 25:10-13 "Then the Lord spoke to Moses, saying, "Phinehas the son of Eleazar, the son of Aaron, the priest, has turned away My wrath from the sons of Israel, in that he was jealous with My jealousy among them, so that I did not destroy the sons of Israel in My jealousy. Therefore, say, 'Behold, I give him My covenant of peace; and it shall be for him and his descendants after him, a covenant of a perpetual priesthood, because he was jealous for his God, and made atonement for the sons of Israel." (See also Psalm 106:30-31)

The Levites Functioned as Israel's Priests

Numbers 8:19 *"I have given the Levites as a gift to Aaron and his sons from among the sons of Israel, to perform the service of the sons of Israel at the Tent of Meeting, and to make atonement on behalf of the sons of Israel...."*

In Genesis 18:22-33, we see how Abraham interceded with God to try to prevent the destruction of Sodom.

Objection # 6: I don't need your Messiah, I already pray and admit My sins to God. I have My own religion.

Is the religion you have in accordance with what the Bible teaches, or is it just what you have traditionally practiced? Are you sure it is the religion that pleases the Lord? Are you sure your confession brings God's forgiveness? Or, do you just hope so? Does your religion bring you into a personal relationship with the Lord? If it does, what is the evidence of that? Do you want to know God in a personal way? If you do, the Bible teaches you the way to enter that relationship.

Objection # 7: Why have Christians hated and persecuted the Jews?

Every true Christian should feel grieved over the persecution which has been inflicted on Jewish people **in the name of Jesus.** (If you are not familiar with this horrific history, I recommend you read my book, **"So Deeply Scarred."**) Also, it is essential to realize that not everyone who claims to be a Christian is one. Even regular attendance at Church services does not make someone a true Christian. Those so-called "Christians" who persecuted the Jews were people who had never experienced spiritual birth and a changed nature. They were merely members of that expression of the religion called "Christianity." Only people who have experienced that spiritual re-birth and had a true heart change that inspires a love for God and for all people, and a desire to obey Jesus as Lord of their lives, are authentic believers.

Jesus commanded His followers to love all people.

Matthew 5:44 *"But I say unto you, love your enemies, bless them that curse you, do good to them that hate you, and pray for them which despitefully use you, and persecute you."*

John 13:35 *"By this shall all men know that ye are My disciples if ye have love one to another."*

CHAPTER 11 – ANSWERING SOME COMMON JEWISH OB-JECTIONS TO JESUS

Galatians 6:10 *"As we have therefore opportunity, let us do good unto all men, especially unto them who are of the household of faith."*

There is a real Devil in the world. Satan, as he is also known, has worked to deceive many people, including those who led the Church into rejecting and persecuting the Jewish people. This was never the will of God. Such people will answer for their crimes against the Jewish people on the Day of Judgment.

Part of Satan's plans to stop the work of God on the earth (Matthew 16:21-23; Luke 8:11-12; John 8:44; 2 Corinthians 4:3-4) was to create this mutual hostility between the Jewish people and the aberrant version of Christianity. God's plan was, and is, to use the true Church, the authentic Body of Christ, to lovingly inspire faith in Jesus among the Jewish people.

Today many Christians are seeking ways to restore their Biblical relationship and responsibility to the Jews, just as there are Jewish leaders who are seeking the restoration of the "Jewishness" of Jesus.

OBJECTION # 8: THE NEW TESTAMENT IS AN ANTI-SEMITIC BOOK

I believe that an unbiased reading of the New Covenant Scriptures shows a prophetic book of love which calls its readers to repentance, spiritual rebirth, faith, and obedience. It is a very Jewish book. As I mentioned in answering Objection #1, everything in it is built upon the Hebrew Scriptures.

It also gives us a historically accurate representation of the Jewish world at that time. There were many diverse groups within Judaism, and they were often quite hostile to one another. The conflicts between Jesus and His followers and the religious leaders of the day are clearly laid out. Their disputations were simply part and parcel of the way Judaism operated in that day. The Dead Sea Scrolls give ample evidence of this as they speak in very negative terms about the Temple priesthood, condemning them as "Sons of Darkness." In fact, inter-religious disagreements among the various streams of Judaism continue to this day. For example, Orthodox Rabbis in Israel do not recognize the "conversion" of Gentiles into Judaism performed by Conservative or Reformed Rabbis.

The prophetic language that the writers of the New Testament use is no different than the language of the Hebrew prophets. Jesus' strong rebukes to the Jewish leaders of His day is exactly like the prophets' and Moses' himself. They all had extremely strong words for those who rebelled against God, rejected their prophetic ministry, were hypocrites, and who abused their authority.

For example, Isaiah rebukes the Istaelites calling them *"a rebellious people, false sons, sons who refuse to listen to the instruction of the Lord"* (Isaiah 30:9). In even stronger language he calls their leaders *"rulers of Sodom"* and the people, *"people of Gomorrah"* who *"call evil good, and good evil"* (Isaiah 1:10; 5:20). Moses rebuked the people many times, calling them *"stubborn"* and *"rebellious"* (Deuteronomy 9:24; 31:27). God calls the Jewish people *"stiff-necked"* (or obstinate) (Exodus 32:9). Is the God of Israel anti-Semitic?

All the strong rebukes by Israel's prophets that we read throughout the Hebrew Scriptures must be understood against the background of God's deep and eternal love for His people. In Isaiah 49:15-16, God describes His feelings for the Jewish people in this way: *"Can a woman forget her nursing child, and have no compassion on the son of her womb? Even these may forget, but I will not forget you. Behold, I have inscribed you on the palms of My hands; Your walls are continually before Me."*

In Zechariah 2:8, God says that the Jewish people are the *"apple (literally pupil) of His eye."* This is a very loving term of endearment that God does not use for any other nation. In Jeremiah 31:3-4, *"The Lord appeared to him from afar, saying, "I have loved you with an everlasting love; therefore, I have drawn you with lovingkindness. "Again, I will build you, and you shall be rebuilt, O virgin of Israel!"*

CHAPTER 11 – ANSWERING SOME COMMON JEWISH OBJECTIONS TO JESUS

In Jeremiah 31:35-37 God declares that His love for, and commitment to, the Jewish people are as eternal as the Sun, Moon, and Stars, regardless of their behavior.

"Thus says the Lord, who gives the sun for light by day, and the fixed order of the moon and the stars for light by night, who stirs up the sea so that its waves roar; the Lord of hosts is his name: "If this fixed order departs from before me," declares the Lord, "then the offspring of Israel also shall cease from being a nation before me forever." Thus says the Lord, "if the heavens above can be measured, and the foundations of the earth searched out below, then I will also cast off all the offspring of Israel for all that they have done, declares the Lord."

Yes, their sins bring God's judgment and punishment. But that is not intended for rejection or destruction, annihilation or extermination (which is what Satan wants) but to discipline them and call them to repentance, spiritual renewal and rebirth (Leviticus 26:44-45; Deuteronomy 4:26-31, 35-36; 2 Chronicles 30:9; Proverbs 10:17; Ezekiel 36:26-28). The New Testament book of Hebrews which was written specifically for Jewish believers, echoes this principle, *"No discipline seems pleasant at the time, but painful. Later, however, it produces a harvest of righteousness and peace for those who have been trained by it"* (Hebrews 12:11).

God's great love for the Jewish people is seen throughout the miracle-working ministry of Yeshua Himself (Matthew 9:36; 14:14; Mark 6:34). When He prophesied the coming destruction of Jerusalem and the great suffering the people would endure, He felt great lament because of the depth of His desire to gather the people to Himself, but they refused (Matthew 23:37; Luke 13:33).

The apostle Paul is often accused of being "anti-Semitic," especially for the frustration he expressed with the Jews who resisted his ministry in 1 Thessalonians 2:14-16. But Paul, who was once a zealous Pharisee, always affirmed his Jewish identity (Acts 21:39; 22:3; 26:5), declared that he would choose to become *"accursed and separated from the Messiah"* for His people's sake (Romans 9:3). This great Jewish apostle was expressing the same heart that Moses had when he interceded for the rebellious children of Israel, *"Forgive their sin, and if not, please blot me out from Your Book, which You have written!"* (Exodus 32:32-33).

Paul strongly warned Gentile Christians against becoming *"arrogant toward the Jewish people"* because as he taught, they are *"beloved because of God's covenant with the Patriarchs"* and that their *"gifts and calling are irrevocable"* (Romans 11:18, 28-29). In fact, he told the believers that their attitude toward the Jewish people should be one of gratitude, humility, and mercy because they have received mercy from the God of Israel.

Some say that John's gospel is anti-Semitic. But it begins by saying that God chose to become flesh by being born as a Jew in Israel. If John was anti-Semitic he would not have written this, nor would he have recorded Jesus' own words that *"salvation is from the Jews"* (John 4:22). This Gospel was written after the destruction of the Temple in Jerusalem when the Jewish rejection of Jesus was formalized as the unequivocal position of the Jewish leadership. Here we see presented a clear confrontation and choice between loyalty to the Jewish people or obedience to the Jewish Messiah. This confrontation and choice continues to this day. What is more important, the people, or their King?

The word "Jews" in the New Testament can refer to the entire Jewish population, to the Jews who lived in Jerusalem or Judea or just to the Jewish leaders and their immediate followers. It is used to describe the *"moneychangers"* and those who were *"buying and selling in the temple"* who made the *"House of Prayer"* into a *"house of merchandise"* and a *"robbers' den"* (Matthew 21:12-13; Mark 11:15; John 2:13-16), as well as those who believed that Yeshua was the Messiah (Luke 23:37; John 2:23; 7:41; 8:30-31; 10:42). One must read the context carefully. There are many wonderful things that the New Testament has to say about the Jewish people and the wonderful future God has for his ancient "Chosen People" (John 4:22; Romans 3:1-2; 9:1-5; 11:26-27).

While it is true that some Jewish leaders and people were complicit in the betrayal and death of Jesus, it was certainly not the entire Jewish

CHAPTER 11 – ANSWERING SOME COMMON JEWISH OBJECTIONS TO JESUS

population. This is not to mitigate the responsibility of those leaders and their followers. The preaching of the apostles to the Jewish people makes this very clear. The apostle Peter declared that the leaders of the nation and those who conspired with them, though they *"acted in ignorance,"* did in fact *"reject the Holy and Righteous One," "nailing Him to a cross by the hands of godless men,"* and are culpable for *"killing the Author of Life"* whom *"God then raised from the dead"* (Acts 2:23; 3:14-18; 7:52).

It is extremely important to remember that the suffering of the Messiah as an atonement for humanity's sins, and His rejection by the Jewish leadership, was all according to the preordained plan of God (Isaiah 53; Psalm 22:12-18; John 3:16; Acts 2:23; 1 Corinthians 15:3; Revelation 13:8). Jesus declared that *"no one could take His life"* as He voluntarily surrendered Himself to be *"The Lamb of God who takes away the sins of the world"* (John 1:29, 10:14-18; Luke 24:27; Acts 3:18; 26:22; 1 Peter 1:20). He also asked God to forgive His betrayers and executioners because they did not know what they were doing (Luke 23:34).

It is extremely important to understand that it is only the enemies of God's purposes for the Jewish people who blamed all Jews everywhere for all time for the death of Jesus. Calling Jews "Christ Killers" was a demonically inspired lie that was used as a justification for perpetrating satanically inspired evil persecutions. There is no place in the New Testament where the Church, or individual Christians, are called to be instruments of judgment and punishment. Everything done in the Name of Jesus to harm the Jewish people was in absolute disobedience and direct contradiction to the clear teaching of the New Testament. Christians are called to be a people of *"love and good works"* (1 Corinthians 13; Matthew 5:16; Ephesians 2:10; 1 Timothy 6:17), who are *"ambassadors of reconciliation"* that reflect and represent God's love and desire for all people to enter His Kingdom.

Everything done by the so-called "Church" in the "Name of Jesus" that is in opposition to these fundamental truths is built upon Satanically inspired deception and lies.

Let me state this as clearly and as concisely as I can, "Christian" and all other sources of anti-Semitism are demonic!

OBJECTION # 9: WHY ARE YOU TRYING TO CONVERT US? WE HAVE OUR OWN RELIGION! PREACH TO YOUR OWN PEOPLE! THEY NEED IT!

It is the Love of God that inspires all true Christians to tell all people, Jews and Gentiles, about His amazing offer of Salvation and Redemption. Remember this is not about "converting" anyone but inviting them to come into a relationship with the God of Israel. (Isaiah 43:10-12; 44:8; Matthew 28:19-20; Acts 1:8)

All true Christians have been called by the Lord to "preach the Good News" to the Jew first, and then to the nations (Romans 1:16). This Good News, the Gospel of the Jewish Messiah, has become the *"Light to the Nations"* that Isaiah spoke of (Isaiah 42:6; 49:6). This *"Light,"* the message and reality of the resurrected Messiah, Jesus, has changed lives around the world for almost two thousand years.

Judaism, as it has been practiced since the destruction of the Temple, the Priesthood and the Sacrificial system, is a religion created by the Rabbis. It is based on substituting what God said in the Torah He required for atonement with what they have devised and declared to be acceptable replacements. The Rabbis declared: "Prayer, repentance, and charity avert the evil decree." If that was all God required, why would He have created such a precisely detailed and elaborate sacrificial system, with a Temple, Priesthood, and Animal Blood, for providing atonement?

If one's virtue, piety, and religious observance can save one's soul, then the New Covenant Scriptures' revelation of Yeshua's atoning death and resurrection mean nothing. But, and that is a "but" with eternal ramifications, if one's "good works" do not bring eternal salvation, and you reject God's *"free gift of salvation, based on His loving grace and mercy, not on your good works"* (Romans 6:23;

Ephesians 2:4-5, 8), then you stand before a Holy and Righteous God trusting in the wrong thing.

Of course, no one knows how God will judge each life, but are you willing to risk your eternal destiny on how "good" you believe you are? How will God, from whom nothing is hidden, measure your life?

Please consider carefully this thought. If you don't want God in your life now, why would God want you in His Heaven then?

OBJECTION # 10: HOW CAN YOU BELIEVE THAT THE BIBLE IS THE WORD OF GOD?

Jesus believed the Hebrew Scriptures were inspired and claimed they prophesied His coming.

Matthew 5:18 *"For truly I say to you, until heaven and earth pass away, not the smallest letter or stroke shall pass away from the Law, until all is accomplished."*

Luke 16:17 *"But it is easier for heaven and earth to pass away than for one stroke of a letter of the Law to fail."*

John 5:46 *"For if you believed Moses, you would believe Me; for he wrote of Me."*

John 10:35 *"... the Scripture cannot be broken,"*

The Apostle Paul believed that the Old Testament is the Word of God.

2 Timothy 3:15-17 *"All Scripture is God-breathed and is useful for teaching, rebuking, correcting and training in righteousness, so that the man of God may be thoroughly equipped for every good work."*

In referring to Biblical prophecies, the Apostle Peter wrote:

1 Peter 1:25 He also declared that *"The Word of the Lord abides forever, and this is the Word which was preached to you."*

2 Peter 1:21 *"No prophecy was ever made by an act of human will, but men moved by the Holy Spirit spoke from God"*

The Bible itself claims to be the Word of God.

"Thus says the Lord" occurs over four hundred times in the Old Testament.

"God said" occurs forty-two times in the Old Testament and four times in the New Testament.

"God spoke" occurs nine times in the Old Testament and three times in the New Testament.

"The Spirit of the Lord spoke" through people in 2 Samuel 23:2; 1 Kings 22:24; 2 Chronicles 20:14.

The Bible is a book of amazing unity.

The Bible is a compilation of sixty-six individual books that were written in three different languages over a period of approximately 1,500 years. It was written by more than 40 authors from 13 different countries who came from many diverse backgrounds (poets, kings, shepherds, farmers, and priests). Every subject they wrote about shows astounding agreement in purpose and theme. It does not contradict itself theologically, morally, ethically, doctrinally, scientifically, historically, or in any other way. This is a great testimony to the divine inspiration of its writers.

The Bible is unique among all ancient manuscripts.

The number and accuracy of ancient copies of the Scriptures show how precisely they have been transmitted throughout history. This is

CHAPTER 11 – ANSWERING SOME COMMON JEWISH OBJECTIONS TO JESUS

unique among all ancient literature. While this does not prove that the Bible is the Word of God, it does show us that the Scriptures we have today are precisely what was written so long ago.

The Bible and History

Whenever the Bible details historical events, its truthfulness and accuracy have been authenticated by both archeology and other historical sources. All ancient archaeological and manuscript evidence prove the Bible to be the best-documented book from the ancient world. It is because the Bible accurately and truthfully records historically verifiable events that we can confidently trust its message of God's love and eternal purposes for humanity.

It is also interesting to note that the Bible teaches us that the earth *"hangs on nothing"* (Job 26:7) and that God sits on the *"Circle of the earth"* (Isaiah 40:22). How did Job and Isaiah know these things? By divine inspiration.

Biblical Prophecies

The Bible is the only book in the world that has 100% accurate prophecy. As you have already seen, we have shared some of the over three hundred precise prophecies that speak of Jesus as the Messiah in the Old Testament that are fulfilled in the New Testament. As you study Biblical prophecy, you will find hundreds of detailed prophecies relating to the future of individual nations and all of humanity.

We are watching Bible prophecy be fulfilled before our eyes as we witness the restoration of the nation of Israel and the regathering of Jews from every nation to their ancient homeland. Moses warned the Jewish people that the consequences of their sin would be national expulsion (Leviticus 26:14-39 and Deuteronomy 28:15-68). He and the prophets also declared that God would not allow them to be destroyed through death or assimilation. A promised remnant would remain alive and be restored to their ancient homeland. This regathered remnant would rebuild their ruined cities and cultivate their land (see for example: Leviticus 26:44-45; Deuteronomy 30:1-10; Isaiah 11:12; 35:1, 58:12; 61:4; Jeremiah 16:14-15; 29:14; 31:35-37; Ezekiel 36:33-35; 38:8; Amos 9:14-15).

In 1900 there were only about 20,000 Jews in what was then called "Palestine" by the Jews themselves. (Back then no Arab wanted anything to do with "Palestine," nor did they consider themselves "Palestinians"). Today there are 6 million Jews living in Israel.

There simply is no natural way to explain the fulfilled prophecies in the Bible except that they are of divine origin.

The Bible has a unique authority and ability to transform people's lives.

The Bible says that God's Word *"is a lamp to our feet and a light to our path."* (Psalm 119:105). It gives us instruction (the Hebrew word for instruction is "Torah") for living in right relationship with God and each other. Its veracity, power and ability to transform lives is attested to by untold millions throughout history. The Holy Spirit makes the Word of God alive for us and imparts God's peace, love, and joy into our soul. His Word helps us find His plans and purposes that give our lives meaning and significance. The Bible can transform lives because it is God's Word.

The indestructibility of the Bible

The Bible teaches us that we are in a spiritual war and that there really is a devil. Jesus taught us that Satan always tries to "steal" the Word of God before it can take root in our lives (Matthew 13:19). More than any other book, the Bible has been vilified, rejected, demeaned, dismissed, and even destroyed. Roman emperors, communist dictators, atheistic professors and so-called liberal politicians, to name just a few, have all tried to destroy or remove the Bible from influencing society and culture. They have all failed. The Bible is still the most widely translated and published book in the world.

CHAPTER 11 – ANSWERING SOME COMMON JEWISH OBJECTIONS TO JESUS

Although the Bible has been ridiculed as mythology, archeology has confirmed its historical events as accurate. Mocked and scorned as primitive and outdated, its teachings, when obeyed, always have a positive redemptive influence on individuals, societies, and cultures.

No matter how much it is rejected, it remains a fixed light shining into the darkness of sin and suffering. Its ability to withstand every attack is a powerful testimony to the fact that the Bible is truly God's Word and is supernaturally protected by Him. It is, as Jesus said, (once again asserting His deity) *"Heaven and earth will pass away, but My words will never pass away"* (Mark 13:31).

OBJECTION # 11: HOW DO YOU KNOW THERE IS LIFE AFTER DEATH?

King Solomon knew it.

Ecclesiastes 12:7 *"The dust will return to the earth as it was, and the spirit will return to God who gave it."*

King David believed it.

2 Samuel 12:23 *"But now he is dead, wherefore should I fast? Can I bring him back again? I shall go to him, but he shall not return to me."*

Job proclaimed it.

Job 19:26-27 *"Even after my skin is destroyed, yet from my flesh, I shall see God; Whom I myself shall behold, and whom my eyes shall see and not another."*

The Psalmist believed it.

Psalm 9:17 *"The wicked shall be turned into hell, and all the nations that forget God."*

The prophet Isaiah declared it.

Isaiah 26:19 *"Your dead men shall live, together with my dead body shall they arise. Awake and sing, ye that dwell in dust: for your dew is as the dew of herbs, and the earth shall cast out the dead."*

The prophet Daniel proclaimed it.

Daniel 12:2 *"And many of them that sleep in the dust of the earth shall awake, some to everlasting life, and some to shame and everlasting contempt."*

Jesus taught it.

Matthew 22:30-32 *"For in the resurrection they neither marry, nor are given in marriage, but are like angels in Heaven. But regarding the resurrection of the dead, have you not read that which was spoken to you by God, saying, 'I am the God of Abraham, and the God of Isaac, and the God of Jacob'? He is not the God of the dead but of the living."*

John 5:28-29 *"Do not marvel at this; for an hour is coming, in which all who are in the tombs shall hear His voice, and shall come forth; those who did the good deeds to a resurrection of life, those who committed the evil deeds to a resurrection of judgment."*

The Apostle Paul declared and explained it.

Acts 24:15 *"...there shall certainly be a resurrection of both the righteous and the wicked."*
1 Corinthians 15:21-22 *"For since by a man came death, by a man also came the resurrection of the dead. For as in Adam all die, so also in Christ all shall be made alive."*

1 Corinthians 15:42-55 *"So also is the resurrection of the dead. It is sown a perishable body, it is raised an imperishable body; it is sown*

CHAPTER 11 – ANSWERING SOME COMMON JEWISH OBJECTIONS TO JESUS

in dishonor, it is raised in glory; it is sown in weakness, it is raised in power; it is sown a natural body, it is raised a spiritual body. If there is a natural body, there is also a spiritual body. So also, it is written, "The first man, Adam, became a living soul." The last Adam became a life-giving spirit. However, the spiritual is not first, but the natural; then the spiritual. The first man is from the earth, earthy; the second man is from heaven. As is the earthy, so also are those who are earthy; and as is the heavenly, so also are those who are heavenly. And just as we have borne the image of the earthy, we shall also bear the image of the heavenly.

Now I say this, brethren, that flesh and blood cannot inherit the kingdom of God; nor does the perishable inherit the imperishable. Behold, I tell you a mystery; we shall not all sleep, but we shall all be changed, in a moment, in the twinkling of an eye, at the last trumpet; for the trumpet will sound, and the dead will be raised imperishable, and we shall be changed. For this perishable must put on the imperishable, and this mortal must put on immortality. But when this perishable will have put on the imperishable, and this mortal will have put on immortality, then will come about the saying that is written, "Death is swallowed up in victory. "O death, where is your victory? O death, where is your sting?"

OBJECTION # 12: WHAT ABOUT THOSE WHO HAVEN'T HEARD THE GOSPEL? WHAT ABOUT ALL THE VIRTUOUS JEWISH PEOPLE WHO DON'T BELIEVE IN JESUS?

We are not the judge of anyone's eternal destiny. God knows the heart and the deeds of everyone and will judge everyone accordingly (Proverbs 24:12; Romans 2:6-8; Revelation 20:12). The Scriptures teach us that God is both loving and righteous and will judge the world with equity (Genesis 18:25; Psalm 7:11; 9:8; 98:9).

We only know what has been revealed to us in the Bible. We have a responsibility to share the Good News of the *"Free gift of Salvation in the Messiah"* (Romans 6:23; 10:15; Ephesians 2:8) and warn people about the *"Day of Judgment"* when everyone will give an account of their lives (Daniel 7:9-10, 22; 12:2; Acts 17:31; Romans 2:16; 2 Corinthians 5:10).

The message of the Gospel is that we cannot trust our own *"good works"* to get us into Heaven because we all *"fall short"* of the standards of God's righteousness (Romans 3:23). When we believe that God made Jesus' death to be the *"atoning sacrifice for our sins"* (1 John 2:2), the Scriptures declare that we become *"the righteousness of God in Him"* (2 Corinthians 5:21). This is what it means to be *"saved by faith through the gift of the grace of God"* (Ephesians 2:8). This is what makes Jesus our Savior.

God's gracious forgiveness should never be taken as an excuse to sin; God forbid (Romans 6:1-2). His Love and Mercy should be a powerful motive to live an obedient, faithful and fruitful life. This is the way we can express our love to God and thanksgiving for His great gift of salvation and eternal life.

Genesis 18:25 *"Far be it from You to slay the righteous with the wicked, so that the righteous and the wicked are treated alike. Far be it from You! Shall not the Judge of all the earth deal justly?"*

Psalm 96:13; 98:9 *"...The Lord is coming to judge the earth. He will judge the world in righteousness, and the people in His faithfulness.*

OBJECTION # 13: IF I BELIEVE, DO I HAVE TO BE BAPTIZED?

Yes, you need to be baptized, because we are commanded to (Acts 2:38). Please understand that baptism is not a Christian innovation. The word baptize is derived from the Greek word baptizo that means immersion. Ritual immersion is deeply ingrained in Jewish religious tradition and is practiced today mainly by Orthodox Jews. It takes place in a "Mikvah" which means "a collection or pool of water." Since the establishment of the Temple, the Jewish people had been practicing immersion, so they would be ritually clean before entering the Temple area. You can see the remnants of many Mikvahs (Mikvot in Hebrew) that have been unearthed by archeologists when you visit the Southern area of the Temple Mount in Jerusalem.

It was there that the Apostle Peter preached his first sermon after the Holy Spirit fell on the festival of Shavuot (Pentecost) in Acts 2:38-41. He proclaimed that Yeshua was the Messiah to the Jews who had come to Jerusalem to celebrate that "Feast of the Lord" (Leviticus 23:16). When he declared that if they believed they could be "immersed (baptized) in His name and have their sins forgiven, none of the Jews asked, "What is this baptism he is talking about?" as if it was some new "Christian" creation. Baptism is very Jewish! Faith in the Jewish Messiah is very Jewish! Being "immersed" in the "Name of Yeshua the Messiah" is very Jewish!

Conclusion

I believe that any unbiased person who studies the Messianic prophecies of the Hebrew Scriptures will conclude that Jesus/Yeshua is the Messiah. It is also true that an unbiased person may conclude that the prophecies are fulfilled by Jesus, but it never affects their life. There are many Gentiles who "believe" that Jesus is the Jewish Messiah, but never surrender their lives to Him and become His true disciple. Only people who truly encounter the Living God will repent of their sins, surrender their lives to *Jesus as their Lord*, and live to fulfill His plans and purposes. If you have never had such an encounter, I pray that you will!

CHAPTER 12 – SOME GUIDELINES FOR SHARING THE GOOD NEWS ABOUT MESSIAH YESHUA WITH THE JEWISH PEOPLE

When presenting Messianic prophecies, explain how they are fulfilled in Yeshua/Jesus. Explain how Yeshua certainly meets the qualifications and fits the description of the Messiah. If He was not the Messiah, then according to the Jewish Bible, the Messiah must be someone just like Yeshua. He must fulfill all the prophecies we've read, plus others. What are the possibilities for a repeat of circumstances in which a Messiah could duplicate the life and ministry of Yeshua? It is impossible to recreate conditions existing about 2,000 years ago. This would require the birth of Messiah in Bethlehem, rejection by His people, His death to atone for sins, and then His resurrection. Remember, Daniel 9:24-27 declared that the Messiah had to come before the destruction of the Second Temple.

The only intellectually honest interpretation of the historical data and the Hebrew Scriptures is that in fact, Yeshua is the Messiah of Israel.

Build Relationships

Always let your words, expressions and tone of voice, communicate love. Sometimes this is a great challenge, I know, but God will put His love in your heart, and it will then be easy to express it. Don't worry if someone doesn't receive your testimony, that is not your business. Your calling is to share your faith and leave the responses and results to the Lord.

Nobody wants to be preached to. That's like being lectured to as a child. When you get the opportunity to share your faith, do it in a relational way. Try to develop a respectful dialogue that allows for the creation of a relationship in which both of you can share what you believe and why. Find beliefs you may have in common, such as belief in the God of Israel and the Torah. Talk about the "Jewishness" of Jesus and how all the original believers were all Jews.

Talk about your support for the Jewish people, the nation of Israel, and your remorse for the history of "Christian" anti-Semitism. Explain how you understand that your faith in Jesus connects you to the Jewish people and the Jewish roots of your faith. Share how your faith in Jesus gives you a great appreciation and respect for Jewish heritage, traditions and how much you have, and can, learn from the vast treasure of Jewish teaching. Communicate how your faith in the Jewish Messiah is not about joining the Christian religion, but how it has given you a personal relationship with the God of Israel. Explain how Jesus the Jewish Messiah did not come to start a new Gentile religion called "Christianity." He came to open the Kingdom of God to the Nations of the world.

I have found that most people like to talk about what they believe and the things that concern them. The more you get to know a person, the easier it will be to share spiritual truths. As you listen, you will be able to explain what you believe and why you believe it. You can also share your testimony and how the Lord is working in your life.

If it is possible, introduce your friend to other Jewish believers. If that is not possible, introduce them to appropriate websites where they can connect with believing Jews. Meeting a Jewish believer can sometimes create a connection that removes emotional barriers and opens conversations on deeper levels.

Some of the most effective evangelism happens when you're not saying anything and just listening. Listening is one way to show that you care about the other person. So many people have no one who will honestly listen to them. Some people go to professional therapists because they have no one to talk to. I cannot tell you how many times people have told me, "Thank you for listening to me – it has helped me so much." Because that was a very positive experience for them, it created a bond between us.

The secret to effective evangelism is to let the Holy Spirit lead you. As you trust Him to give you wisdom and guidance, you realize that you don't have to have the answer to every question or try to impress people with your knowledge. Pride and arrogance will turn people away from the Lord, but true Godly humility is very attractive.

CHAPTER 12 – SOME GUIDELINES FOR SHARING THE GOOD NEWS ABOUT MESSIAH YESHUA WITH THE JEWISH PEOPLE

Experience, and 1 Peter 3:15, teaches that we should not answer questions that are not being asked. Wait to see where the conversation goes. Listen to their answers to your questions and what questions they may have. You will have a much more fruitful witnessing ministry if you realize that you don't have to know the answer to every question. You can simply say, "That's a good question, I don't know the answer, but I will try to find out." This is also a good time to get permission to contact them for future dialogue.

Be Sensitive to Jewish History and the Holy Spirit

Because the Jewish people have suffered almost 2,000 years of various kinds of persecution from the "Christian Church," the name of "Jesus Christ" and things related to the "Christian" religion have very negative meanings and stir up a deep-seated traditional resistance to the Gospel. (Please see my book on the history of "Christian" anti-Semitism, "So Deeply Scarred.") When we share the Messiah, we must be cognizant of the special areas of sensitivity that have been created by this painful history. To avoid unnecessary conflict, we must learn which words and concepts are particularly volatile and avoid using them.

We want our witness about Jesus to be made in a way that reflects that understanding of historical "Christian" anti-Semitism and is respectful of Jewish religious understanding, culture, traditions, and identity. We must ask the Holy Spirit to enable us to use what we learn so we can be *"wise as serpents and gentle as doves"* (Matthew 10:16) as we talk to Jewish people about their Messiah in a "Jewish" way.

Be careful how you use the word "Jew," because it can have a pejorative meaning attached to it. When a Jewish person hears someone say "Jew," or use the expression "the Jews," they immediately focus on if it is meant in a derogatory way. For example, if you meet someone who you think may be Jewish, don't ask, "Are you a Jew?" It is much better to ask, "Are you Jewish?" Instead of saying "Jews" say the "Jewish people" or the "Jewish Community."

This is much more respectful, and although it may seem like a small change, it carries great positive emotional power.

Remember, words have experiences, memories, and feelings attached to them. There is a great sensitivity to these terms because one painful lesson of Jewish history is that derogatory words have often been the first step to more serious attacks. If you see any negative response to words you use, ask if you said something to make them uncomfortable. This shows that you are sensitive to the feelings of the person you are talking to. Most people will be more open to talk if they know you are sensitive to their feelings.

Never be accusatory or negative. Don't say: "You Jews don't believe the Messiah has come" or "you Jews rejected the Messiah." Be positive; plant positive seeds. Say: "Your Messiah has changed my life." Share the changes that have taken place in your life since you came to faith in Jesus. You can explain that Jesus died for them also and wants to bring them to Himself. This is one way to let your light shine!

As you probably know there is a tremendously rich heritage of Jewish humor. However, it is wise to avoid telling jokes about "the Jews." It is okay for Jewish people to tell jokes about themselves, but many find it offensive when Gentiles tell such jokes because of the concern that anti-Semitism may be lurking behind the humor.

Avoid anti-Semitic terms or ethnic slurs. Of course, ethnic slurs, derogatory expressions, and disdain for any group have no place in the vocabulary of a child of God. We should all be guided by Ephesians 4:29 *"Let no unwholesome word proceed from your mouth, but only such a word as is good for edification according to the need of the moment, that it may give grace to those who hear."*

For example, never use the term "Jew you down" – this is very insulting, as it infers that Jewish people are the only ones who ever negotiate for a better price. Terms like "Jew boy" or "Kike" are extremely offensive. "Kike" is the Jewish equivalent to the "N" word.

CHAPTER 12 – SOME GUIDELINES FOR SHARING THE GOOD NEWS ABOUT MESSIAH YESHUA WITH THE JEWISH PEOPLE

Don't refer to a "Jewish conspiracy." This is another historic accusation that the Jews have already, or are planning to, control the world. Saying things like "you Jews are all the same" or "you know how the Jews are" are also all very insulting.

[By the way, there is a real "Jewish Conspiracy." It is plainly revealed in the pages of the Bible. One day the God of Israel will return the "King of the Jews" to "Rule the world" (Psalm 2, 22:27-31; 110:1-3; Isaiah 2:1-4; 9:6-7; 11:3-9; 24:21-23; 2 Thessalonians 1:7-10; Revelation 19:15-16). There are many more such verses.]

If possible, avoid displaying pictures of Jesus as this can be considered as an idolatrous image (Exodus 20:4). Similarly, avoid displaying or wearing a cross. Because so many Jewish people endured great suffering and were murdered under the sign of the cross, its display provokes deep-seated powerful negative emotions. <u>For the Jewish people, the cross is a symbol of hatred, persecution, and death, not redemption and salvation.</u>

Avoid saying "Jesus Christ." The name "Jesus" and the term "Christ" do not have any "Jewish" connotations, and because of history, their usage also stirs up strong negative feelings and erects emotional barriers. Jesus' Hebrew name is Yeshua, and Christ is a synonym for "Messiah." It is much more "Jewish" to say "Messiah Yeshua" or "Yeshua Ha-Mashiach." Mashiach is the Hebrew word for Messiah ("Ha" means "the"), so Ha-Mashiach means "the Messiah." (Mashiach is pronounced Ma – she – ach). The 'ach' sound is made as if you were clearing your throat.

If you continually use the word "Yeshua" or the phrase "Yeshua Ha-Mashiach," please understand that the Jewish person you are talking to may not understand that you are referring to "Jesus Christ." I heard a story of a Jewish woman who was invited to a meeting to hear about "Yeshua HaMashiach." When she realized that they were talking about "Jesus Christ," she was very angry and left feeling that she was lied to and misled. Never be open to the accusation that you were deceptive. Be very clear who you are talking about. This is extremely important! We are never to be *"ashamed of the Gospel"* (Romans 1:16) or nullify the message of the Cross because it is *"foolishness to those who are perishing, but to us who are being saved, it is the power of God." "Messiah crucified is a stumbling block to Jews and foolishness to Gentiles, but to those who are called, both Jews and Greeks, Messiah is the power and the wisdom of God"* (1 Corinthians 1:17-18, 23-24).

Use the Scriptures

A joke is told of a Gentile who went into a Jewish bookstore and asked for an Old Testament. The clerk said, "How old?" Jewish people do not believe in a "New Testament," so how could they refer to their Bible as the "Old Testament?" They refer to their Bible as the "Tanach." As I wrote earlier, Tanach is another name for the Hebrew Bible. It is an acronym of the first Hebrew letter of each of the three traditional parts of the Bible: **T**orah (literally "instructions") – specifically the first five books of Moses, **N**evi'im (from the Hebrew word for Prophet, Navi) – refers to the Prophets, and **K**etuvim (the Hebrew word for "Writings"), i.e., Job, Psalms, Proverbs, etc. Hence, TaNaKh. You can also refer to the Old Testament as the Hebrew Scriptures or Jewish Bible.

Try to answer questions or objections from the Scriptures. Encourage your friend to study the Bible for themselves, or even with you. If you use a Jewish translation make sure you are familiar with it first. Not only are the books and some verses in a different order than English versions, but the Hebrew is also sometimes translated differently and gives a different meaning to the verse. You can go back to the Hebrew and discuss the various meanings of the words. Most Jewish people are more comfortable with a Jewish translation than a "Gentile Bible." Don't be overly concerned about this. As God draws someone to Himself, He can use any translation to reveal who Jesus really is.

Don't limit the study to Messianic prophecies. The Word of God is very powerful and can change lives as it is simply being read. People are not saved by our rational or intelligent arguments, or by the eloquence of our words. Salvation is a supernatural experience. People are saved by God's grace through faith which is created by God's Word (Ephesians 2:8; Romans 10:17; 1 Peter 1:23).

CHAPTER 12 – SOME GUIDELINES FOR SHARING THE GOOD NEWS ABOUT MESSIAH YESHUA WITH THE JEWISH PEOPLE

We can confidently pray for those we share the Gospel with because God said that *"He would watch over His Word to perform it"* (Jeremiah 1:12). He also said, *"So shall My Word be which goes forth from My mouth; It shall not return to me empty, without accomplishing what I desire, and without succeeding in the matter for which I sent it"* (Isaiah 55:11). Always remember that *"the Word of God is living and active and sharper than any two-edged sword, piercing as far as the division of soul and spirit, of both joints and marrow, and able to judge the thoughts and intentions of the heart"* (Hebrews 4:12).

One Holy Spirit anointed verse, or even something you share can become a life-changing revelation for someone if God is drawing them to faith in His Son. Remember what Jesus taught in John 6:44, *"No one can come to Me unless the Father who sent Me draws Him,"* and He repeats it for emphasis in verse 65, *"I told you that no one can come to Me unless it has been granted him from the Father."*

Choose Your Words Wisely

Here is a list of words you can use when sharing the Gospel with the Jewish people that have more of a "Jewish" connotation and will generally not cause an immediate negative response. It would be wise to familiarize yourself with this list and use it prudently. However, it is important to understand that none of the words I suggest you avoid are "bad" words in and of themselves. They all can have wonderful Godly meanings. But because of historical "Christian" anti-Semitism, for many Jewish people, they have negative emotional baggage attached which you need to be aware of. Please understand that these are only guidelines to be used as you are led by the Holy Spirit. Don't be in bondage to them. If the Lord leads you to use a particular word, do so. God knows how He will use what you share. Don't limit God, and of course, be led by the Spirit.

Instead of	**Use**
Jew(s)	Jewish/Jewish people/Jewish community
Christian	Believer
Christ	Messiah\Mashiach

Jesus	Yeshua
Church	Congregation\Assembly
Gospel	Good News
Saved	Came to faith
Convert	Become a believer
Missionary	Messenger
Born Again	Born from Above, or New Heart or New Spirit (Ezekiel 11:19; 36:26)
Completed Jew	Jewish Believer or Messianic Jew
Holy Ghost	Holy Spirit or Ruach HaKodesh (Hebrew for Holy Spirit)
Old Testament	Torah, Tanach or Jewish Bible, Hebrew Bible or Hebrew Scriptures
New Testament	New Covenant or Brit HaDashah (Hebrew for New Covenant)

The power of your testimony

Sharing your salvation testimony is a very powerful witness of the reality of God. People can argue theological interpretations of Biblical texts, but they cannot argue with your experiences. Of course, they can dismiss them for a variety of reasons. Do not be discouraged if they do. Pray that the Lord will use your story to bring them to faith.

Share miraculous answers to prayer in your life. You never know how those stories can affect someone. As you share, pray that it will provoke them to spiritual jealousy. If someone says something like, "I wish I had your faith," you can share that God wants them to have it also and that the message that creates faith is found in the Bible. This would be a good opportunity to give them a Bible or even just a New Testament as you encourage them to open their heart as they read it.

I have found that an excellent resource to create is a small tract that has your personal testimony. Put your picture or something appropriate on the cover. A good outline to follow is that the first part should be something of your life before you met the Lord. Then share how you came to faith. The last part should tell how your life has

CHAPTER 12 – SOME GUIDELINES FOR SHARING THE GOOD NEWS ABOUT MESSIAH YESHUA WITH THE JEWISH PEOPLE

changed since then. Don't dwell too much on the sins of your past. Don't put in too many details. The point of the tract is to focus on Jesus, not how bad or sad you were. Keep the tract short and to the point or it is likely the person won't bother to take the time to read it.

If you want to share your testimony with Jewish people, remember to use words that reflect your understanding of how Jewish people "hear" certain words.

Please don't think that you don't have a very "good" testimony. Every life changed by the love and grace of God is a powerful witness. Everybody who has been "born again" has a story to share. Don't let the devil demean you. You never know how what happened to you can profoundly impact someone else.

If you don't think you can write it out, then sit with someone and record your testimony. Then find someone to transcribe and edit it. If you're a good writer, then maybe you can start a ministry (or small business!) recording, transcribing and editing personal testimony tracts!

I have discovered that when people begin to read your life story, they tend to believe it is true. As you hand it to them, you can simply say, "This is what happened to me." When I do that with my own tract, people take it and begin to read.

Pray for Those to Whom You Witness

Always offer to pray for those you share the Gospel with. Many times, people who are not open to discussing spiritual things or reading the Bible will be open to prayer. God always seems to be particularly pleased to honor those prayers as evidence of His existence. Even if people refuse to pray with you, you can pray for them privately or with other believers and *watch God work* (Matthew 6:6).

It is never acceptable to press someone to pray to receive the Lord; however, when someone understands the Gospel and is ready to repent of their sins and receive Jesus as Lord and Savior, ask them if they would like to. Don't assume people know what to do with their openness to the Lord. Some people just need an invitation. Give it to them. Lead them in a prayer of repentance and receiving the Lord Jesus into their lives!!

CHAPTER 13 – EXPLAINING THE GOSPEL TO THE JEWISH PEOPLE

There are spiritual principles for a relationship with God taught in the Bible. If you want to have a personal relationship with God, you must understand that:

God wants us to enjoy life with Him as we become His children and His disciples and fulfill His plans for our life.

Psalm 16:11 *"You will show me the path of life: in Your presence is fullness of joy; at Your right hand there are pleasures for evermore."*

Psalm 37:23-24 *"The steps of a man are established by the Lord, and he delights in His way. When he falls, he shall not be hurled headlong; Because the Lord is the One who holds his hand."*

Jeremiah 31:3 *"The Lord appeared to him from afar, saying, "I have loved you with an everlasting love; Therefore, I have drawn you with loving-kindness."*

John 10:10 *"I came that they might have life and might have it abundantly."*

If you want to have a personal relationship with God, you must understand that God is Holy and Righteous.

Leviticus 19:2 *"Speak unto all the congregation of the children of Israel, and say unto them, you shall be holy: for I the Lord your God am Holy."*

Psalm 92:15 *"The Lord is upright; He is My rock, and there is no unrighteousness in Him."*

Simply stated, humanity is sinful and separated from God. Sin is a spiritual barrier that prevents us from experiencing God's love and His plans for our life.

You must understand that all have sinned.

Ecclesiastes 7:20 *"Indeed, there is not a righteous man on earth who continually does good and who never sins."*

Isaiah 64:6 *"For all of us have become like one who is unclean, and all our righteous deeds are like a filthy garment, and all of us wither like a leaf, and our iniquities, like the wind, take us away."*

Psalm 53:2-3 *"God has looked down from heaven upon the sons of men, to see if there is anyone who understands, who seeks after God. Every one of them has turned aside; together they have become corrupt; there is no one who does good, not even one."*

You must understand that God won't allow sin in His presence.

Psalm 5:4-6 *"For You are not a God who takes pleasure in wickedness; No evil dwells with You. The boastful shall not stand before your eyes; You hate all who do iniquity. You destroy those who speak falsehood; The Lord abhors the man of bloodshed and deceit."*

Numbers 14:18 *"The Lord is longsuffering, and of great mercy, forgiving iniquity and transgression, and by no means clearing the guilty, visiting the iniquity of the fathers upon the children unto the third and fourth generation."* (Unrepentant sin carries into future generations, i.e., children learn sinful ways from their parents).

You must understand that sin causes a separation and creates a barrier that keeps us from God.

Isaiah 59:2 *"But your iniquities have made a separation between you and your God, and your sins have hidden His face from you so that He does not hear."*

You must understand that the penalty for sin is death.

Ezekiel 18:20 *"The person who sins will die. The son will not bear the punishment for the father's iniquity, nor will the father bear the*

CHAPTER 13 – EXPLAINING THE GOSPEL TO THE JEWISH PEOPLE

punishment for the son's iniquity; the righteousness of the righteous will be upon himself, and the wickedness of the wicked will be upon himself." (Everyone is responsible for their own words, choices, and behavior).

Romans 6:23 *"For the wages of sin is death, but the free gift of God is eternal life in Messiah Yeshua our Lord."*

You must understand that you cannot remove your sin by your own efforts.

Psalm 143:2 *"Enter not into judgment with your servant: for in your sight shall no man living be justified."*

Psalm 49:7-8, 15 *"No man can by any means redeem his brother or give God a ransom for him. For the redemption of his soul is costly." "But God will redeem my soul from the power of the grave: for he shall receive me. Selah."*

Psalm 51:1-2 *"Have mercy upon me, O God, according to your loving-kindness: according to the multitude of your tender mercies blot out my transgressions. Wash me thoroughly from mine iniquity, and cleanse me from my sin."*

You must understand that the sin barrier can be removed by believing that Messiah's death on the Cross is the Sacrifice that makes Atonement for your sins.

Jesus' death is the fulfillment of all the Old Testament sacrifices. They all were temporary. They prophetically pointed to the shedding of Messiah's atoning blood.

Leviticus 17:11 *"For the life of the flesh is in the blood, and I have given it to you on the altar to make atonement for your souls; for it is the blood because of the life that makes atonement."*
Leviticus 10:17 *"... the sin offering ... is most holy, and God has given it to you to bear the iniquity of the congregation, to make atonement for them before the Lord."*

Leviticus 4:27-35 *"And if any one of the common people sin .... then he shall bring his offering ... for his sin... and the priest shall burn it upon the altar for a sweet savor unto the Lord, and the priest shall make an atonement for him, and it shall be forgiven him. ... And the priest shall make an atonement for his sin that he has committed, and it shall be forgiven him."*

Isaiah 53:3-6 *"He was despised and forsaken of men, a man of sorrows, and acquainted with grief; and like one from whom men hide their face, He was despised, and we did not esteem Him. Surely our griefs He bore, and our sorrows He carried; yet we esteemed Him stricken, smitten of God, and afflicted. But He was pierced through for our transgressions; He was crushed for our iniquities; the chastening for our well-being fell upon Him, and by His scourging, we are healed. All of us like sheep have gone astray, each of us has turned to his own way, But the Lord has caused the iniquity of us all to fall on Him."*

You can receive Messiah Yeshua into your life as Savior and Lord by faith.

John 1:11-12 *"He came to His own, and those who were His own did not receive Him. But as many as receive Him, to them He gives the right to become children of God, even to those who believe in His name."*

When you receive Him, He causes you to have a spiritual re-birth.

John 3:5-7 *"Jesus answered, Truly, truly, I say to you, unless one is born of water and the Spirit, he cannot enter into the Kingdom of God. That which is born of the flesh is flesh, and that which is born of the Spirit is spirit. Do not marvel that I said to you; you must be born again."*

1 Peter 1:3 *"Blessed be the God and Father of our Lord Jesus the Messiah, who according to His great mercy has caused us to be born again to a living hope through the resurrection of Jesus from the dead ...."*

CHAPTER 13 – EXPLAINING THE GOSPEL TO THE JEWISH PEOPLE

1 Peter 1:23 *"For you have been born again not of seed which is perishable but imperishable, that is, through the living and abiding word of God."*

You can pray right now wherever you are!

You can pray in your own words. There is no formula to follow. God knows your heart and is not concerned with your exact words, but rather with the attitude of your heart. The following is just a suggested prayer:

"Lord God of Israel, I believe that Yeshua/Jesus is the Messiah and your Son. I believe that He died as an atonement for My sins. I believe that He rose from the dead and will one day return to rule the earth from Jerusalem. Yeshua, I ask you now to come into My heart, come into my life and cause me to be spiritually reborn. Lord, please fill me with your Holy Spirit, so that I might have the power to obey you and do your will and be the person you want me to be. God of Abraham, Isaac, and Jacob, I pray all of this in the Name of Yeshua, your Son, and My Savior. Amen!"

How to grow as a believer:

G – Go to God in prayer every day (John 15:7).
R – Read the Bible every day (Acts 17:11).
O – Obey God as best you can (John 14:21).
W – Witness for Yeshua by your words and how you live (John 15:8).
T – Trust God with every aspect of your life (1 Peter 5:7).
H – Holy Spirit – allow Him to lead and empower you (John 14:16-17; 15:26; 16:7-15).

It is important to join a good Church or Messianic Congregation. We were not designed by God to be alone in our spiritual life. We need to be part of a "Community of Faith." There you can meet others to help you learn, change, and grow in your relationship with the Lord.

My prayer is that you will use what you have learned in this book to become a faithful witness of the Messiah to the Jewish people. I also pray that those Jewish people you share with will have a life-changing encounter with the God of Israel and His Resurrected Messiah! Amen!!

RESOURCES

Messianic Prophecy/Jewish Evangelism Books
Messianic Prophecy, by Arthur Kac.
The Messianic Series by David L. Cooper, available for free download at www.biblicalresearch.info.
All the Messianic Prophecies of the Bible by Herbert Lockyer.

By Michael Brown:
Answering Jewish Objections to Jesus, 5 Volumes.
The Real Kosher Jesus.
What Do Jewish People Think About Jesus?
Sixty Questions Christians Ask About Jewish Beliefs and Practices.

By David Baron:
Types, Psalms, and Prophecies: A Series of Old Testament Studies.
Rays of Messiah's Glory: Christ in the Old Testament.
The Servant of Jehovah: The Sufferings of the Messiah and the Glory That Should Follow.

By Risto Santala:
The Messiah in the New Testament in the Light of Rabbinical Writings.
The Messiah in the Old Testament in the Light of Rabbinical Writings.

Jewish Evangelism Websites
Askdrbrown.org
Chosenpeopleministries.org
Jewishvoice.org
JewsforJesus.org
OneforIsrael.org
SidRoth.org (Messianic Vision Ministries)

CONTACT INFORMATION

Howard Morgan Ministries
www.HMMin.com

In the US
PO Box 956486
Duluth, Ga 30096
770-734-0044
info@HMMin.com

In the UK
0151-652-9956
Karen@HMMin.com

In Canada
250-816-0543
Corina@HMMin.com